EVIDENT EQUITY

A Guide for

Creating

Systemwide

Change in

Schools

LAURYN MASCAREÑAZ

Solution Tree | Press
a division of
Solution Tree

555 North Morton Street
Bloomington, IN 47404
800.733.6786 (toll free) / 812.336.7700
FAX: 812.336.7790

email: info@SolutionTree.com
SolutionTree.com

Visit **go.SolutionTree.com/diversityandequity** to download the free reproducibles in this book.

Printed in the United States of America

LCCN: 2021040144

Solution Tree
Jeffrey C. Jones, CEO
Edmund M. Ackerman, President

Solution Tree Press
President and Publisher: Douglas M. Rife
Associate Publisher: Sarah Payne-Mills
Art Director: Rian Anderson
Managing Production Editor: Kendra Slayton
Editorial Director: Todd Brakke
Copy Chief: Jessi Finn
Production Editor: Miranda Addonizio
Acquisitions Editor: Sarah Jubar
Content Development Specialist: Amy Rubenstein
Copy Editor: Mark Hain
Proofreader: Kate St. Ives
Text and Cover Designer: Laura Cox
Editorial Assistants: Sarah Ludwig and Elijah Oates

For Grandma June.
Your love and laughter live on.

ACKNOWLEDGMENTS

This book draws from a well of knowledge that goes much deeper than me and my own education and experiences. I draw from generations of antiracist educators, activists, and researchers who paved the way for me. I acknowledge my ancestors, living and passed, who crossed borders and who survived borders that crossed them, who both assimilated and defied culture, culminating in my unique identity and opportunity to live and learn and teach in this country.

First, to my mom, Robyn, who was one of the early advocates for culturally responsive teaching and learning and who, along with her students, exemplified what they should look like: Your classrooms were my incubator for social justice and equity. The kindness you showed to your students and families, the lunch dates and home visits and integration of their cultures into your curriculum, were the examples I leaned on and tried to replicate when I was teaching. You showed me how to care and fight for people and issues outside myself; from you, I learned that being a teacher extends far beyond the classroom walls. Thank you for this foundation, for being the person and educator you are. I am who I am because of you.

To Landon: your presence is a gentle shadow in every one of my life's memories. You are my first and best friend, and I follow in your footsteps of greatness and purpose. Together, we are healing the generations that we come from and paving a bright path for the ones who will one day trace their lineage and read our stories. Fortune favors the bold, and we are worth every prayer whispered by our ancestors.

To Daddy: you are without a doubt my biggest fan and the first person I want to call when good news happens (and when things go wrong). I am humbled by the well of love you have for me. I am proud to once again prove you right. Hearing your laughing voice telling me "I told you" is all the motivation I need to keep going. Your pride in me is like a thousand suns on my heart.

To Sarah Jubar, the patron saint of book editors, who appeared in my email in-box one random January day: without you, this book (literally) would never have happened.

To the Office of Equity Affairs team and my coalition in Wake County, North Carolina: Rodney, Mama Teresa, Christina, Cecelia, Rosa, Granvel, Pam, Ryan, Char, Kristen, Terrance, Jan, Roxann, Dan, Kim, Phil, Sara, Doug, Kelly, Susie, Molly, Crystal, Bria, and countless others: I love you all and am so proud to do this work alongside you. So much of this book was born from the trial by fire of our first three years together and the result of the wisdom, strength, and care you all have shown me.

To more than three hundred students, "my kids": being your teacher is one of the greatest honors of my life, and I miss being in the classroom with you all every day.

To three incredible women: Val Ortega, Tamitrice Rice-Mitchell, and Mindy Bolar, the leaders who hired me, believed in me, and pushed me both professionally and personally.

To my professors in the Ethnic Studies Department at the University of Colorado, Boulder, including the late, great Adrian Gaskins: learning from you as a young person shifted my entire worldview, and I am eternally grateful.

To my OG (original) Teaching Tolerance team: Gabe, Hoyt, Jarah, Lindsey, Jey, Monita, Steffany, Julia, Madison, Margaret, Michelle, Colin, and Shannon, I learned so much about this important work and even more about life from spending my days, nights, and weekends with all of you in the Deep South.

To Adrienne, my #AuthorClub partner and the eye of every hurricane: your calming energy and persistence in seeing the humanity in ourselves and others is one of the major drivers in my own ambition to create a better world.

To Sara: a very eager and naïve young teacher timidly approached you and said, "I want to be you when I grow up." Your kind heart listened and gave me the chance to change the course of my life. There are not enough words for the gratitude I have, and I still hope to be you when I grow up.

To Cory: thank you for reminding me why I wanted to write a book when things were hard. One text or video call from you is all I ever need to be reminded of all that is good in the world.

To Annie and the entire Vandy crew: you carried me through the doctoral process and never fail to hype me up and keep me laughing.

To Daniela, RJ, Kristin, Gretchen, and Brandie: you are the most supportive and powerful group of women, and I am humbled by your love and friendship through my struggles and success.

To my Mascareñaz and Miller families, my friends, and countless colleagues and peers and mentors who have inspired me and cheered me on along the way: you may not be listed individually here, but know that I hold each of you close and lean on you to bring me through each day.

And last on this list but first in everything I do, to my son, Jack Thomas. When you were born, it was almost like you knew that our journey would be a trying one; through each move and transition, you have remained resilient and happy. In the first five years of your life, we have been through so much together, and I am grateful for your imagination, your empathy, your flexibility, and your deeply kind and sensitive heart. You have an intuitive sense of justice and are not afraid to stand up for yourself and others. I do this work so that you may grow up in a school system ready to recognize your brilliance and a world that will see you for the beautiful person you are. I love you times infinity.

Solution Tree Press would like to thank the following reviewers:

Scott McLeod
Associate Professor of Educational
  Leadership
University of Colorado Denver
Denver, Colorado

Kathy Perez
Professor Emerita, Author,
  International Consultant
Saint Mary's College of California
Alameda, California

David Pillar
Assistant Director
Hoosier Hills Career Center
Bloomington, Indiana

Dawn Vang
Assistant Principal
McDeeds Creek Elementary
Southern Pines, North Carolina

Steven Weber
Associate Superintendent for Teaching
  and Learning
Fayetteville Public Schools
Fayetteville, Arkansas

Dianne Yee
Superintendent, School Improvement
Calgary Board of Education
Calgary, Alberta

Visit **go.SolutionTree.com/diversityandequity** to download the free reproducibles in this book.

TABLE OF CONTENTS

ABOUT THE AUTHOR

 **Lauryn Mascareñaz, EdD** (she/her/hers), is the former director of equity affairs for Wake County Public Schools in Wake County, North Carolina. She is a career educator who spent ten years as an elementary classroom teacher and instructional coach in Denver, Colorado, and the Bay Area of California. Her passion for culturally responsive instruction also led her to Learning for Justice (formerly Teaching Tolerance), a project of the Southern Poverty Law Center, where she served as a teaching and learning specialist. Lauryn is inspired by the equity-minded educators she works alongside each day and is particularly dedicated to closing the opportunity gap for young males of color.

Lauryn works with school stakeholders as a consultant to strategically plan their equity work and confront roadblocks that are unique to their communities. She believes in using antiracist pedagogy and critical race theory to address institutional inequities. As a presenter, she's toured the United States, speaking on topics ranging from antibias curriculum and courageous conversations about race to leading for systemic equity.

Lauryn holds a bachelor's degree in American and ethnic studies and a master of education degree in language, literacy, and culturally responsive teaching, both from the University of Colorado, Boulder and Denver respectively. She earned her doctor of education degree in leadership and organizational systems from Vanderbilt University.

To learn more about Lauryn's work, visit www.risedei.com, or follow her on Twitter @laurynmaria.

To book Lauryn Mascareñaz for professional development, contact pd@Solution Tree.com.

INTRODUCTION

Equity work is not the next best thing—it is *the* thing. It is the lens through which we as educators and citizens see everything in our society. I liken it to a journey; and no matter where you are in your equity journey, you are a part of the system of education, and your learning can make a difference. It is neither another curriculum nor professional learning. It cannot be reduced to a few hours of work or a checklist. Instead, equity work is a state of mind and a set of values; it is how we talk to people and how we see students and families. It is about creating a counternarrative to the way things have always been done and challenging the status quo. When an educator complains about a student by saying, "He is always late," equity stops to look deeper before it asks, "Why doesn't he want to go to class?" Equity is inclusive and states "our students" instead of "those kids." Equity centers students and families and shouts, "Their families love them and want the best for them" instead of "*They* don't value education like we do."

I once heard an educator note that we can't talk about equity in schools until we talk about how schools were never meant to be equitable in the first place. The bold simplicity of this statement struck me. I had never heard this said so plainly. Indeed, as far back as the late eighteenth century, Thomas Jefferson (1814) proposed two tracks of learning in the United States: one for the laboring (to qualify them for their pursuits and duties) and one for the learned (as a foundation for further acquirements). The learned track was for those who could in the future conduct "the affairs of the nation" (Jefferson, 1814). For generations, Black, Latino/a, and Indigenous students were barred from any form of formal schooling and faced serious repercussions for becoming literate (Race Forward, 2006).

There is a long history in education of disproportionality in discipline data between White and Black, Indigenous, and people of color (BIPOC) students, institutional bias against groups that have been marginalized, and curricula steeped in Whiteness and colonialism (Benson & Fiarman, 2020; Peters, 2015; Riddle & Sinclair, 2019; Scialabba, 2017). A deeper focus on education's collective history, beyond *Brown v. Board of Education* (the 1954 U.S. Supreme Court ruling that decreed state laws establishing racial segregation in public schools are unconstitutional), helps shed light on the state of schools in the 21st century. The narrative of the racial achievement gap in the United States and many other countries, including Canada and Australia, is steeped in centuries of racism and oppression in schools that didn't end with formal integration but have further perpetuated division in our collective communities (Hinkson, 2015; Orfield & Eaton, 1997).

A report by the Equity and Excellence Commission (2013) tells us that "the inequities within the U.S. education system impose an economic impact on the country equivalent to a 'permanent national recession.'" The report goes on to state:

> Ten million students in America's poorest communities—and millions more African American, Latino, Asian American, Pacific Islander, American Indian and Alaska Native students who are not poor—are having their lives unjustly and irredeemably blighted by a system that consigns them to the lowest-performing teachers, the most run-down facilities, and academic expectations and opportunities considerably lower than what we expect of other students. These vestiges of segregation, discrimination and inequality are unfinished business for our nation. (Equity and Excellence Commission, 2013)

In addition to these wealth inequities, we also see how inequities in the education system lead to lack of support (resulting in alarming statistics such that LGBTQ+ students are three times more likely than others to contemplate suicide; Centers for Disease Control and Prevention, 2016), and contribute to phenomena such as the school-to-prison pipeline, a term that describes how Black, Brown, and Indigenous boys are disproportionately incarcerated (American Civil Liberties Union, n.d.).

While these issues are not new, our approach to addressing them can be. We can create intentional and strategic change that can make big impacts on our students lives and futures. That is what this book is for—to guide you, wherever you are in your equity journey, to bring about this change.

The long path of racial and cultural change in our school systems has been ever evolving—ranging from initiatives on integration, to multiculturalism, to diversity, and now to equity. The arc toward educational social justice and true opportunities for all students is now actively antiracist work. Malini Ranganathan (as cited in North, 2020), a faculty team lead at the Antiracist Research and Policy Center at American University, says that *antiracism* involves "taking stock of and eradicating policies that are racist, that have racist outcomes, and making sure that ultimately, we're working towards a much more egalitarian, emancipatory society." We see school districts of varying sizes creating positions or offices focused solely on the work of antiracism, diversity, equity, and inclusion. Yet this work is still new and revolutionary in its approach.

Historically, the emphasis in our education system was how to add programs, people, or materials in order to create an equitable outcome for students. The problem with this is that we cannot add equity to a system that is inherently inequitable. I refer to this as *sprinkling equity*: it's impossible to take something that is created on a foundation of inequity and then sprinkle a little diversity training or one-time cultural night on top of it and expect different outcomes. Instead, the emphasis must be on analyzing and reconstructing the system—while we are a part of it. For instance, if course enrollment procedures always lead to disproportionate numbers of students having access to these courses, you cannot merely add more advanced course offerings. You have to shift and change the process for how students are assigned to these courses.

How do we navigate this course? How do education leaders who work toward equitable schools know where to start, who their allies are in this work, and what battles to fight? We must understand that changing systems requires a multifaceted approach. There is no one fix in this work and no specific starting point or strategy that will work for all. Peter M. Senge and John D. Sterman (1992), in their landmark research on systems thinking, remind us that "the more profound the change in strategy, the deeper must be the change in thinking" (p. 1007). Researchers Susy Ndaruhutse, Charlotte Jones, and Anna Riggall (2019), in their report on systems thinking for the Educational Development Trust, conclude that the holistic approach of systems thinking offers a way not only to enact sustainable change but to do so more quickly than by taking things piecemeal. This can be true of education outcomes and deeper systemwide change. *Evident Equity* works to show leaders how to analyze their own systems and processes to identify areas for change while also reflecting on their own identity as equity leaders.

Without a doubt, equity work is isolating and brutal; it is a position that demands countless hours in front of large audiences talking about the most sensitive and taboo subjects in our society: bias, stereotypes, race, religion, sexuality, and more. It involves constantly gut checking your own values and beliefs about students, education, and privilege. Equity work requires an endless well of hope and optimism for a better future even when you are faced daily with the dark and divisive outcomes of our past, such as racism, bigotry, and homophobia. There will also be those who ascribe equity to a political party or who see your advocacy for all students as a roadblock to success for their own families. Yet here we are. The hope and optimism we share as educators brought us to the classroom and will aid us in our equity journey too.

This book will provide a framework to help you in this equity leadership position and apply change in four different areas of your school or district: (1) systems, (2) shared learning, (3) teams, and (4) environment. We will look at how and why we must consider all four areas when seeking educational equity. But before I explain who will benefit from reading this book, what material you can expect from the chapters to come, the goals of this book, and the type of future we can build with the knowledge and tools herein, I'd like for us come to a shared understanding of the concept of equity.

EQUITY DEFINED

According to the National Equity Project (n.d.), *equity*, as I use the term in this book, refers to eliminating the predictability of success and failure that currently correlates with any number of social and cultural factors, such as race, language, and geographic location. Equity in education includes the process of interrupting inequitable practices such as discipline disproportionality and gifted and advanced placement, challenging biases, and creating inclusive school environments for all intersections of identities, including gender, race, ethnicity, and citizenship status. In fact, the Organisation for Economic Co-operation and Development (2012) explains, "Equity in education means that personal or social circumstances, such as gender, ethnic origin or family background, are not obstacles to achieving educational potential" (p. 37).

Often, I have heard equity boiled down to "differentiation" in educator speak. When educators differentiate, they are designing their instruction according to individual needs. But if we are differentiating and not specifically seeking to increase the achievement of, amplify the voices of, and improve outcomes for those who have been oppressed, then we are not truly engaging in equity work. This is one way that equity differs from equality. Equity is about taking into account all the historical and present-day factors that are barriers to access and then removing them. Equality is about creating the same access for everyone, regardless of historical and current factors like institutional racism and bias.

The umbrella of equity is large and encompasses multiple identities. It includes the LGBTQ+ community, refugees, immigrants, students experiencing poverty and homelessness, students learning English, students in the juvenile justice system, and more. Although racial equity is often at the forefront of this work, we must force ourselves to see that people are intersectional by nature and that our current education systems do not fully protect or support those who have been historically marginalized. For instance, let's look at a student who identifies as Latina. This part of her does not make up her entire identity. She may also be unhoused (experiencing homelessness) or a part of the LGBTQ+ community. This intersection of identities means that this student must deal with mounting pressure as a result of multiple marginalized identities, which is in essence what *intersectionality* describes: the ways that social categorizations interconnect to create overlapping disadvantages.

Tool

See https://youtu.be/w6dnj2IyYjE for a great primer video on intersectionality. As educators who aspire to be equitable, we must be attuned to the multiple aspects of oppression our students are experiencing.

Earlier education initiatives focused on tolerance and acceptance, such as multicultural and diversity policies. For example, in Québec in the 1980s, multiculturalism became a federal policy that centered around celebrating and sustaining cultural diversity (Brosseau & Dewing, 2009). In the post-1960s, Civil Rights Movement–era United States, a growing body of scholarship led by James Banks advocated for an education system that focused on educational equality (Gorski, 1999). As the landscape of education changes, the conversation has shifted into equity and antiracism, which instead advocate for large-scale systemic change that directly addresses the social justice implications of education. There is no precedent for this. Equity-minded educators in North America and worldwide are navigating their own unique contexts, histories, and circumstances.

ABOUT THIS BOOK

This book serves as a tool for educators who wish to critically analyze the structures they are working within with the goal of creating more systematically equitable schools for all students. It does so by exploring four areas educators can focus on as they map out equity work at the school or district level. Figure I.1 depicts each of these areas as quadrants in what I call the *equity heat map*.

Organizational Equity	Shared Equity
Get close and get specific.	Build a coalition and build capacity.
What are the top-down systems and structures within your organization that you can change?	Who are your allies, and how can you learn together in order to enact change?
Structured Equity	**Evident Equity**
Work the system.	Live it out.
What equity shifts in process and goals can you make to teams and groups that are already in place?	In what ways is equity evident in your environment: walls, signage, messaging, curriculum choices, and more?

Figure I.1: Equity heat map.

The equity heat map came about as a result of a conversation I had with a colleague about the equity work she was doing at her school. My team and I in the Office of Equity Affairs spent each day out in our district working with schools and conducting professional learning and coaching sessions. We expressed our shared frustration that schools were creating equity teams, but school and district leaders often reached out to us for support because the culture and environment of the schools were not shifting. I started scribbling ideas for how to help equity leaders see equity as something beyond a team or committee. The idea of it being a heat map came about during a team conversation; we realized schools and departments could use the quadrants to map the equity work they were doing already and identify "hot" and "cold" spots. For instance, a school could list all the equity teams it has, which would make the structured equity square hot. But if that's all that school has done, the rest of the areas would still be cold, showing how much work is yet to be done. When we reduce this work to a mere team, we severely undervalue its power within our schools and larger society. Surely teams, as groups of people who meet in person or virtually to accomplish goals, are an important part of an equitable school system, but they are just that—a *part* of it. An equitable school system includes building a coalition and creating and sustaining equitable systems, structures, and environments. After a chapter overview, I'll discuss who this book is for and its goals.

Chapter Overview

Each of the book's first four chapters details one quadrant of the equity heat map. Chapter 1 lays out how we can work toward organizational equity, a process that must begin by homing in on and getting proximate to both the inequities and the people who experience or negotiate those inequities every day. Chapter 2 delves into shared equity and the ways to build a coalition of people who will support or carry out the equity work. Chapter 2 also discusses the essential process of gauging staff's readiness to embark on this undertaking and planning thoughtfully so that everyone stays within a zone of productivity rather than succumbs to frustration or exhaustion. Chapter 3 explores structured equity, in which we collaborate with existing school teams to ensure all staff work is equity centered. In chapter 4, we'll acquaint ourselves with evident equity as a way of making certain that equity is indeed evident in school and district spaces.

Each of these four chapters includes:

- Ways in which specific equity work would live out in both school and district settings
- Real-life elementary, middle, and high school examples that show how equity educators have grappled with and had success in this work
- Tools to aid you in the process of your equity work

- Tables for your equity planning
- Reflection questions and key takeaways

Chapter 5 covers how to stand firm in the face of backlash as you move forward. One of the most difficult parts of this work is dealing with stakeholders who are resistant to change, and this concluding chapter will equip you to take on this aspect of the work with intentionality and empathy. There are also appendixes with helpful resources that can offer a springboard for your equity work.

It is important to note that there is no concrete sequence to these areas of work. Some educators may want to focus on structured equity through teams, for example, while others may wish to work on a few concepts in each quadrant. *The goal is to eventually move into a holistic approach to all four quadrants so that you weave equity throughout the fabric of your institution.* If educators remain in one of the quadrants indefinitely, they can never move or reconstruct the system. As you begin to tackle and rewrite policies and structures in each area, you will start the process of a more systematic approach to equity work. Some successful leaders I have worked with have focused on one small aspect from each quadrant at a time, ensuring that they don't overwhelm their staff but also staying consistent in their intention to keep equity at the forefront instead of a side project. The sequence is up to you and your context— you know your site better than anyone.

Who Is This Book For?

This book is for anyone who is leading equity work in schools. To the teacher who is trying to drum up support and make small changes in an environment hostile to change: this book is for you. To the superintendent of a one-school district or two-hundred-school district: this book is for you. To the principals who are bravely leading their staff through incremental and deliberate change and the assistant principals who are taking the reins to create change: this is for you. I wrote this book so that stakeholders from a diverse array of backgrounds and professional titles can use its framework and knowledge in order to drive change in schools.

Goals for This Book

I want this book to serve as a grounding space for best practices, a reflective tool for change, and an easy-to-use resource that will help educators create systemwide change for all students. My hope is that educators will go through their policies, structures, teams, and professional development plans with a fine-tooth comb to re-create them as antiracist. My intention is to be a hopeful and helpful voice to educators who are struggling and feeling alone in this difficult, demanding, but essential work.

LET'S DO THIS

As I complete this book in September 2021, our world is experiencing the intersection of two global pandemics; COVID-19 and systemic racism have changed our reality and laid bare the inequities at the root of our society. The infection and death-rate disproportionality in COVID-19 sickness highlights the generational struggles of Black, Latino/a, and Indigenous families (Centers for Disease Control and Prevention, 2020). As journalist Gillian Brockell (2021) writes, there is ongoing blame and violence toward Asian Americans rooted in racism and xenophobia. The sudden closing of schools and the subsequent landslide of need for daily food, shelter, and financial support have been unlike anything generations of people have ever seen. The inequities of every system in our societies are on full display: in the United States, the unemployment rate reached 14.8 percent in 2020, the highest in recorded history (Falk, Romero, Carter, Nicchitta, & Nyhof, 2021), while from 2020 to 2021 the combined wealth of billionaires went up by 55 percent—$1.6 trillion dollars (Americans for Tax Fairness & Institute for Policy Studies, 2021). Globally, as economies recover from the pandemic, major economies like China and the United States are recording robust growth, while low-income economies like Somalia, Afghanistan, and Niger have seen the slowest economic growth since 2000, directly affecting per-capita income (World Bank, 2021). The long history of racism and marginalization in the United States and around the world continues into the present as communities suffer. Society is holding up teachers as heroes alongside doctors, nurses, and other *essential workers* (a new term in our collective vocabulary) and yet at the same time treating them as babysitters who are disposable in the race to improve our economies.

Writing this in 2021, I am feeling how dark and heavy this time of the pandemic is. I know that it will take us a long time to get back to normal, but I hope that in the race to return to normalcy, we are asking ourselves which aspect of "normal" we want to return to. By the time you read this, I hope that *antiracism* is a widely studied term and that we continue to hold one another accountable to difficult conversations about race and racism. I hope that all our students find themselves in an environment that is inclusive and supportive of their whole, authentic selves and that educators will be standing tall another day, knowing their contributions and time are valued and honored.

Finally, I want to leave you with one more thought. In the summer of 2020, I gathered with equity leaders from across the country on a video call with the incredible author and teacher educator Gloria Ladson-Billings. She spoke with us about the history of nations that rebuilt their education systems after mass casualties and about the necessity of not returning to "school as usual" (G. Ladson-Billings, personal communication, July 9, 2020). She expands on this sentiment in her article, "I'm Here for the Hard Re-Set: Post Pandemic Pedagogy to Preserve Our Culture," urging educators to consider "what kind of human beings/citizens we are seeking to produce" and challenging "educators to engage and interrogate their own worldviews and develop the facility to move from the center to the margins" (Ladson-Billings, 2021).

Before ending the call, Ladson-Billings shared with us the beautiful words of Indian author and activist Arundhati Roy (2020):

> Historically, pandemics have forced humans to break with the past and imagine their world anew. This one is no different. It is a portal, a gateway between one world and the next. We can choose to walk through it, dragging the carcasses of our prejudice and hatred, our avarice, our data banks and dead ideas, our dead rivers and smoky skies behind us. Or we can walk through lightly, with little luggage, ready to imagine another world. And ready to fight for it.

Let's rise. Let's imagine that other world and continue to fight for it.

1

ORGANIZATIONAL EQUITY
Get Close and Get Specific

If you are willing to get closer to people who are suffering, you will find the power to change the world.

—Bryan Stevenson

Those of us working at the district or administrative level are passionate about education and students, but the reality is we are a step removed from the classroom. We make decisions and attend meetings all day long, so we must work even harder to keep our why close to our choices and our work every day. Student outcomes are what we are here for—our business is students' academic, social, emotional, and physical growth. When we keep this in mind, the changes that we need to make become even clearer. But knowing that we need to make change to best serve *all* our students and knowing *where to start* are two very different things. In this chapter, we'll discuss how you can look at the top-down systems and structures within your organization. Let's explore how to get proximate, get specific, and ultimately make organizational change.

GET PROXIMATE

Between 2016 and 2018, while I was creating professional development and writing curricula for the Southern Poverty Law Center in Alabama, I was fortunate enough to work down the street from activist and civil rights lawyer Bryan Stevenson and his incredible organization, Equal Justice Initiative (www.eji.org). Stevenson often spoke at different events around town, and knowing his work for prison reform and the National Memorial for Peace and Justice, I took every opportunity to see him speak.

At an Alabama State University event, he spoke about the power of being proximate. *Proximate*, as he described it, is about one's proximity to the inequity that is occurring. For Stevenson, it meant visiting prisons all over Alabama to spend time talking with the people who he was defending.

At the time, I struggled with this very concept, as I felt so far away from what was actually happening in schools. I was part of a team committed to helping teachers and school administrators incorporate antibias and antiracist practices into their schools and classrooms. After many years of being a teacher, for the first time in my career, I was removed from the day-to-day equity work of instructing, planning, and spending time with students—so much so, in fact, that I was unsure about the audience and result of our efforts. Instead of holding face-to-face trainings with teachers and having conversations with them, we delivered our professional development via webinar or website. Our online messaging and outreach revolved on a news cycle, leaving us reactionary in nature. Only a few of us had actually spent any real time as teachers. In short, we were severely out of touch with what was happening in classrooms each day.

Stevenson (as cited in Fernandez, 2016) believes that "if you are willing to get closer to people who are suffering, you will find the power to change the world." As I heard him say this at Alabama State University, I scrambled to add this message to the notes section of my phone. Later, I sat with those words for some time. How could I get more proximate? My position as a teaching and learning specialist for the Southern Poverty Law Center offered me the ability to reach thousands of educators through an email or article, but I didn't have my finger on the pulse of what educators wanted or needed to hear. To offer a solution, I created a memo for my team about how the power of proximity could serve our mission. Our nonprofit had an endowment that allowed us to dream big, so my plan included in-person professional development all over the United States: a new city each month, about two hundred educators, and our small team. The outpouring of interest was immediate, our audience was hungry for in-person learning with the team, and we were able to hire some brilliant trainers who were adult-learning experts. The relative logistical challenge of planning these professional developments (including flights, hotels, and materials) ended up being small in comparison to the impact they had on our mission to support educators in being antibias and antiracist.

Spending time in close proximity to teachers meant we had to rewrite curricula and build meaningful relationships with a huge network of like-minded educators. Stevenson's words and example were the impetus to understanding that I had to be in physical space with our audience in order to understand and develop the mutual respect needed to grow as educators. Teachers told us they needed more usable materials richer in action and fewer focused on theory. Administrators told us they wanted accessible, in-person training for their teams in order to capitalize on interest and passion around certain topics. We listened to the feedback and made changes accordingly. The professional developments around the country continued to sell out each training as new cities were added each month and even resulted in the expansion of the nonprofit to include a full-time, on-the-ground group of trainers. Educators from around the country were now ordering materials to conduct professional development with their own staff and creating public-facing lesson plans on our website that incorporated social justice tenets. This experience comes to mind often for me now that I work in a district office. In order to keep current with what our educators and students need, we must be proximate. Here are a few ideas for what that might look like at the school or district level.

At the school level, you can:

- Conduct student or community open forums

- Ensure department heads or team leaders have standing time to share feedback and voice their concerns

- Encourage administration (and staff!) to spend time in classrooms, hallways, and all common spaces in order to build authentic relationships with students and each other; these relationships will lead to open dialogue and a clearer understanding of what is happening in the school.

At the district level, you can:

- Make certain a wide representation of teachers provides feedback on training

- Ask a diverse array of staff with various job roles what topics *they* are interested in, then use those data to drive professional development offerings

- Encourage district office staff to spend time in the school car pool, recess, after-school activities, and lunchrooms at least once a month; see chapter 3 (page 43) for examples of how one district did this with success.

Getting proximate allows us to build organic, trusting relationships. It is easy to fall out of touch with what is happening with our communities if we are not directly *in* community with them. For me as a teacher, this meant going to some of my students' sporting events. I could show up as an adult who cared about them, and they saw that I had a relationship with their coach and families where we could all talk without the weight of titles and roles we each had in a school setting.

GET SPECIFIC: FIND YOUR HARBOR

Lucius Annaeus Seneca (1920), a Hispano-Roman Stoic philosopher, statesman, and dramatist, once said, "Our plans miscarry because they have no aim. When a man does not know what harbour he is making for, no wind is the right wind" (p. 75). We must start our equity work with a goal in mind. Often, we are so overwhelmed by the number of tasks ahead and by the need to determine what harbor we are headed for that we just start throwing everything but the kitchen sink at our teachers and students in the hope that something sticks. Leadership often ends up being like Oprah in a giveaway episode: "You get a team! You get a curriculum! You get a training!"

But hold up. First, we need to consider what we are trying to achieve. We can't just start equity initiatives without a full sense of what we are ultimately hoping to achieve. Once you have your goal, you can build backward. As teachers, we would start with what we want our students to learn. Then, we would design lessons to meet that goal. The same process of planning works in equity leadership. Some examples of questions to help drive your goal setting could be these: What do you want your teachers to be able to do differently or understand more deeply? How do you want your students to feel about the culture of the school? The answers to these questions are your destination, your harbor.

Think about sitting down a year from now. What will you hope has changed at your site between now and then? After working through this question, equity leaders will often organically land on a goal they feel will be most impactful for their specific site. Here are a few examples of equity goals.

- Uncovering a connection between teacher bias and student discipline, such as a gender disproportionality in referrals for the same behavior

- Fostering authentic cross-cultural relationships with students and families that go beyond parent-teacher conferences

- Increasing instructional engagement for BIPOC students using culturally responsive pedagogy

- Establishing clear guidance for how to approach subjects of gender and sexuality, such as pronoun expectations for staff and students

- Finding ways to decease the opportunity or achievement gap within a particular subgroup by talking directly to the students in that subgroup

You may have a team you can work with collaboratively to determine your harbor, or you may be on your own to determine what your next steps will be. You may want to use school or district surveys, standardized test scores, suspension data, and other sources to aid in answering some of the following questions. It helps to define which inequities are "personal, local, and immediate" (Singleton, 2015, p. 28). That is, what is within your locus of control? Poverty may indeed be an inequity that our students are facing, but it is not within the control of one school or district to make a goal to disrupt the system of poverty. Instead, you may want to consider how the effects of poverty manifest inside your school and district (think about access to food, supplies, field trips, and so on) and use those as focus areas instead.

With your team or individually, try working through some of the reflection questions in figure 1.1 to help you best pinpoint what your equity focus could be. The questions are sequential, so start at the top and work your way down.

Reflection Question	Response
What inequities are present at our site?	
Think about where we would like to be one year from now and complete the prompt "I want my staff to be able to. . . ."	
Which of the present inequities are within our control? For example, poverty is not within our sphere of control, but access to free or reduced lunch may be.	
Which identified inequities have the greatest impact on our students? On our school culture?	
What are one or two goals for change that align with these inequities?	

Figure 1.1: Reflection questions for setting equity focus goals.

*Visit **go.SolutionTree.com/diversityandequity** for a free reproducible version of this figure.*

Leaders in both school and district positions often have a gut reaction when having a coaching conversation to determine their equity harbor. Sometimes, they are ready with their area of focus even before a coaching conversation can occur. Whether leaders can express this area of focus out loud or in quiet reflection when responding to guiding questions, many times they have a strong sense of what needs to be achieved. However, that might not always be the case. And that's not a bad thing. Often, we must determine that the ripeness of the issue—or readiness for change—is not there yet.

Maybe the school just shifted leadership, and the new administration needs time to take stock of everything. Or perhaps the district is undergoing serious fiscal or organizational roadblocks. In these cases, enacting change and setting goals may not be the best course of action. In these types of scenarios where more data and time are needed, equity audit tools can be useful. Equity audit tools give you a comprehensive look at your school or organization and can provide a large- or small-scale view of what exactly is happening in your school or district environment. They can include walkthroughs, surveys, checklists, and listening sessions.

Tool

Mid-Atlantic Equity Consortium has a massive equity audit tool package that is free and can be tailored to your school or district. Visit https://maec.org/resource/equity-audit-materials/ for more information.

MAKE ORGANIZATIONAL CHANGE

Schools and districts are organizations. They are built with hierarchies of responsibilities and separated into areas of expertise. One way we can call out inequity is through addressing top-down systems and structures that may seem as though they are inherently part of the organization. These are the processes and protocols that feel like they have "always been done this way" and have become institutionalized. These institutional systems, as scholars Rita Kohli, Marcos Pizarro, and Arturo Nevárez (2017) note, have "replaced the overt and blatant discriminatory policies and practices of the past with covert and more subtle beliefs and behaviors, reflecting the persistent and pervasive nature of racism" (pp. 184–185). An example of one of these systems at the school level would be class lists; while schools are no longer officially segregated based on race, the processes that class lists are based on can still be biased against the well-being of marginalized communities. At a district level, an example would be hiring and recruitment techniques; while it's illegal to discriminate during the hiring process, discrimination does still occur because the ways that schools often recruit and hire new teachers can shut out nondominant groups. Policies like these are ripe for an antiracist approach. Let's take a closer look at these examples as models for how to assess and shift processes and protocols in order to make organizational change.

Tool

Equity Impact Analysis Tool (Race Forward; https://bit.ly/3s9G0gX)

This tool from Race Forward is accessible online and is a framework that provides a series of questions to ask when a proposed action is on the table. It prompts leaders to ask: "Who does this proposed action serve? Who does it not serve?"

School-Level System—Class Lists

In schools, *class lists*—determining which students will be assigned to which course or teacher—come to be through multiple processes and procedures. Teachers may gather to create them together, a computer-based algorithm may combine students into grade-level alike classes, such as equally sorting all students in the fourth grade, or teacher recommendations may come into play and students are instead hand-placed. But let's look deeply at the ramifications of class lists.

We know that racial isolation in schools—such as placing the few Latino/a students in a grade level in different classes on their own rather than combining them together in one class—is detrimental to both the academic and social-emotional well-being of BIPOC students. In one study, researchers Andy Sharma, Ann Moss Joyner, and Ashley Osment (2014) show that attendance at a racially isolated school is associated with quantifiable and statistically significant lower performance for Black students on both algebra and English end-of-course exams. Additionally, work by senior research consultant Nancy McArdle and human development and social policy scholar Dolores Acevedo-Garcia (2017) indicates early education "segregation also squanders a particularly fruitful time during child development and an environment that could be potentially ideal for fostering intergroup contact necessary for developing healthy racial attitudes." Racial isolation, however, is a sensitive subject and is likely rare in conversations when creating class lists. We'll discuss examples of how to handle class lists at the elementary, middle, and high school levels.

Elementary School Example

After being introduced to the equity heat map (see figure I.1, page 5), a colleague of mine grappled with how class lists would fit into an equity focus. She was a brand-new principal at a majority-White school with a very small population of BIPOC students. In her conversations with me, it became clear that her equity focus had landed on establishing a more inclusive environment for her BIPOC population. She was thinking of shifting the norm that a new student always be added to the class with the least number of students. She felt classes should be balanced more for individual student needs, but she was worried that teachers might feel as though she was being unfair or that their workload would be disproportionately or inordinately increased.

Ultimately, she decided to shift the procedure of her site so that when a new student entered the school, she would consult with her data manager to view a racial breakdown of each classroom. This would be done to avoid racially isolating any one student. She spent time at a staff meeting explaining the reason behind her decision and provided her staff with the research base to back up her recommendation. The next time a student enrolled, the data manager pulled the numbers and the student was placed in the classroom that would best serve that student's academic *and* social-emotional success. This is a prime example of how equity is not equality. It's about what is the best class for each individual student (equity) and *not* about the same number of students in each class (equality).

Middle School Example

A middle school principal I worked with had identified BIPOC male student achievement as his school's area of focus. As he pored over data, he noticed that BIPOC male students who had reached the mandated test score were not being enrolled in future Advanced Placement (AP) class lists because of lack of middle school teacher recommendation. In fact, the more he dug, the more he saw that the students who were not recommended (but had met the score cutoff) were overwhelmingly Black boys. Now, he knew there was some learning he needed to do with his staff (bias work—pronto), so he planned for that. But he also took it a step further to address, too, the organizational systems in place that had made this inequity possible. In theory, teachers were to report on a recommendation list any student who met a test-score threshold. Teachers had the autonomy to not include students based on their personal views of whether the students could be successful in an AP course. Then, the teachers would give the list to the instructional coach and counselor making class lists. These mandated lists and decisions were the systems that had fed into this educational inequity.

The principal tasked his staff with identifying students who had met or were on the cusp of meeting the set cutoff for enrollment into AP classes. Once they were identified, not only were all the students automatically enrolled, but the 10 percent of students right below that cutoff were also given the chance to enroll. This served to disrupt the system of test scores and teacher recommendations as the only gateway to enter these courses. The system was now open to more students who would not have had access before. This purposeful and deliberate re-examining of enrollment created opportunities for students that did not exist prior. And with staff participating in professional development around the new process and learning about implicit bias, they have successfully disrupted an inequity.

High School Example

As an instructional coach, I used to make class lists with my colleagues in a collaborative team setup. We added mounds of data and acronyms to tiny sticky notes and posted them to a massive whiteboard. It paralleled a football draft in its complexity and the emotions it incited. Teachers would be fired up about making additions to students' sticky notes and claiming that certain students—often BIPOC males—had "behavior issues." In contrast, they were also quick to label Asian students as gifted and talented or as "model students."

Applying an antiracist lens to this process forces us to ask who this process serves and who it does not. Were students who were struggling with discipline issues (a disproportionate number of BIPOC students) given a chance to have a clean slate the next year? Or did this process further exacerbate structural racism and inequity? Were Asian students considered "model minorities," brushing aside their own unique academic strengths and struggles? Consider the impact of this at the high school level: How do we apply this same critical lens of antiracism to our specialized course offerings? Who do AP and honors-level courses serve? Who do they not serve? Many schools serve both magnet and base populations, and you can look at those course offerings similarly. Answering these questions will help us see which students *are* receiving the most rigorous instruction and which students *could* be.

District-Level System—Hiring and Recruitment Techniques

At the district level, making changes in systems may look like evaluating hiring and recruitment methods. Who has access to what kind of jobs in the district? Are applications offered in a variety of different modalities to serve all different types of abilities, or only online through a personal computer? When the district team is recruiting, who goes out into the community and appears at job fairs? Is it a diverse team who accurately reflects the community in which you serve? Further, where does the recruiting take place? If we go to the same places, we will get the same results. We know there is a shortage of BIPOC teachers, according to the U.S. Department of Education (2016)—so do we recruit at nearby historically Black colleges and universities (HBCUs), or do we stick to the same schools of education we have always gone to? Do we intentionally create mentoring and peer groups that support BIPOC teachers in predominately White systems? How about the advertisements and marketing materials our district puts out—is there a diverse representation of teachers in the images?

I discussed with our human resources team our district's intentionality when recruiting talent. The team knew that people want to work somewhere that aligns with their values. We all agreed that the district could be more specific in its messaging about what it stood for and who it was recruiting.

Take a glance at your district's messaging on its job site. What does it say? There is a huge difference between "Come work with us!" and "Join us in our commitment to social justice as we place equity, student achievement, and accountability at the forefront of every child's education." Human resources and talent recruitment may feel far removed from equity work—but think about the impact. Research from Jason Greenberg Motamedi and David Stevens (2018) of the Washington State Vibrant Teaching Force Alliance suggests that students of color who have at least one teacher of color may do better on tests and be less likely to have disciplinary issues. The same research also suggests that White students show improved problem-solving abilities, critical thinking, and creativity when they have diverse teachers (Motamedi & Stevens, 2018). Therefore, antiracist organizational shifts from class lists to talent recruitment can have a lasting positive effect for individual students and classrooms alike.

Top-Down Systems

Top-down systems are mandated policies and procedures that are institutionalized over time by those in positions of power or authority. They could include, for example, a memo from the superintendent about the when, where, and what of staff meetings, a process of approving curriculum changes solidified by a department, or certain routines like bell schedules and car-pool processes that a principal has implemented. Whatever they are, they are different from other systems in that they come from the highest levels of leadership in an organization.

Table 1.1 shows what systems we can look at when making organizational change. The first part of organizational change is identifying the system itself and then thinking of potential actions for change. For leaders, the hard part is how we must move from systems thinking into the process of reconceptualizing complex issues, designing better operating policies, and guiding organization-wide learning (Ndaruhutse et al., 2019; Senge & Sterman, 1992). The table is not exhaustive, but it will provide you with examples of what these systems are within schools and districts and potential actions that you could take in similar situations.

Each system in table 1.1 has been shifted and changed by educators to ensure a more equitable outcome for the member of the school community most affected by that inequity. Using the equity impact analysis tool (see page 16), leaders can ask questions about each system (for example, "Who does this work for?" and "Who does this not work for?") in order to gain insight into how each system can be changed. For instance, in table 1.1, the first school-system action involves the car-pool system for caregivers picking up and dropping off their students. By asking who that system worked for and who it did not work for, the educators I worked with determined that the car pool was for English-speaking parents who had their own transportation and who had jobs that allowed them to pick up and drop off their children. They also determined that the current signage they had available communicated a harsh message rather than a welcoming or inclusive one. By highlighting these findings, the school made an adjustment to its schoolwide car-pool routine to ensure that Spanish-speaking parents who were driving or walking would encounter staff who could greet them in their own language and answer any questions they had (for more best practices in reaching students and families who are learning English, see appendix B, page 81). Another school also updated its signage; figure 1.2 (page 23) conveys the dramatic shift in messaging that assistant principal Timothy Huber was able to create.

Table 1.1: Example of Top-Down School and District Systems

| | | | Organizational Top-Down Systems | | |
| | | | What inequities are present in these systems? | | |
School Systems	Possible Inequity	Example Action	District Systems	Possible Inequity	Example Action
Schoolwide car pool	English-speaking families can interact with and easily ask questions of staff, but non-English-speaking families cannot	Spanish-speaking staff present at car pool or pickup ask parents whether they have any questions or concerns	Policy	No clear stance on equity goals or beliefs	Determine whether district equity policy is present and, if so, whether it is all-encompassing for diverse stakeholders
Class lists	A small population of Latino/a students is distributed throughout a grade	Ensure students from historically marginalized groups are not isolated by grouping them together	Hiring and recruiting methods	Lack of diversity in staffing	Rebrand marketing materials with diverse representation of staff and students; including district equity goals
Attendance and tardy policies	Large number of tardies and consequences given for tardiness during a certain time of the school day or certain period	Analyze data for which period or class students are often tardy, and meet with students to determine why they are not in a hurry to get to said period or what is inhibiting them from arriving on time	Evaluation process	Teachers are underusing culturally responsive pedagogy in their instruction	Include levels of proficiency for culturally responsive pedagogy in expectations
Advanced or honors versus core enrollment	Systems perpetuate White and Asian enrollment in advanced courses	Audit classes for racial groups present in each, and compare to school demographics for potential disproportionality, then create a system that provides equal access and more representative enrollment	Guidelines for LGBTQ+ students	Students who are transgender are dead named (that is, called by their birth name when they have chosen a new one to correspond to their identity) and referred to as wrong gender	Establish district norms for pronoun usage in email signatures, on name tags, and in introductions
Gifted and talented recommendations and services	Systems perpetuate White and Asian enrollment in gifted and talented programs	Walk through process from beginning to end through the perspective of a non-English speaker, those experiencing poverty, an underrepresented subgroup, or a special education student to see whether access is universal	Equity mapping and audit tools	Staff and departments create their own audit or find different tools online, resulting in disparate measures and levels of outcomes	Provide district-approved equity audit tools and aligned professional development for school and department leaders

continued ▶

School Systems	Possible Inequity	Action Example	District Systems	Possible Inequity	Action Example
Special education recommendations and services	Parents are not able to fully understand or grasp special education plans and legal jargon	Special education staff meet with parent advocacy groups and liaisons to determine best ways to work with parents and help them understand special education goals and legalities	Disability access for and accommodations for work spaces	Staff and community who are deaf or hard of hearing cannot access important announcements or emergency signals	Install flashing lights in tandem with intercom systems for deaf and hard-of-hearing community
In-school-suspension classrooms	In-school suspension is regularly full to overflowing	Staff team meets to determine schoolwide expectations for what behaviors necessitate in-school suspension and ensure they are universally held to in service of checking bias and reducing discipline disproportionality	Important communication updates for families and caregivers	Families without technology or who are learning English are out of the loop for important messages and updates	District updates are sent via text, email, phone message, or other preferred medium in the family's home language
Access to building	People who are differently abled cannot easily get into and out of the building	Principal meets with building and facilities personnel to assess school grounds' openness to differently abled bodies and skills (for example, Braille signage, ramps, and playground swings for wheelchair users)	District leadership meetings	Diversity, equity, and inclusion department or single staff member is the sole advocate for equity concerns inequity	Co-create team agreements that address how to hold difficult conversations about race and other sensitive subjects
Homework	Students cannot independently complete task or understand skill and do not have access to an adult or caregiver to help them	Implement alternative supports during the school day for all students to complete assignments and ask for help in lieu of homework	Professional development model and offerings	Staff have widely variant skills and competencies when approaching instruction and pedagogy	Provide baseline training for all staff on district-established core competencies and how they align to district vision or strategic plan
Report cards	Student grades do not include commentary or adjoining resources to help caregivers understand what grades mean	Grade-level teams meet to establish norms for report card comments with clear, actionable feedback for student growth	Cultural or religious support	The district only celebrates major Judeo-Christian holidays and offices are decorated in Christmas-centric themes	Distribute a calendar that highlights major holidays of multiple religions, offers relevant background information and details on where to learn more, and outlines workplace implications for time off and possible accommodations

Old sign:

Updated sign:

Figure 1.2: A shift in messaging from harsh to inclusive.

This is not only an example of how we can create changes in systems like car-pool routines and pick-up and drop-off procedures but also of how equity can be evident in the environments we live and work in (see chapter 4, page 59, for more about evident equity) through something as simple as signage.

I have co-created the list in table 1.1 over time with colleagues and peers in this work to show a glimpse into what other equity leaders grapple with. As you move forward in your equity journey, you will undoubtedly find new systems that fall into organizational change that you will need to address to provide equitable outcomes for students.

CONCLUSION

In this chapter, we've recognized the critical importance of getting close, or proximate, to inequity—those who experience it and those who observe it—to better appreciate the needs and perspectives of our stakeholders and build relationships characterized by trust and open communication. After we listen to those experiencing inequity and reflect on their unique observations, it's time for stocktaking and starting equity work with the end in mind: what is it that we ultimately want to achieve? Unless we can get specific about our goals, we may derail our own well-intentioned efforts. Finally, once we get both proximate and specific, we can start to think more critically about our institutional systems, and who benefits or suffers by the very design of our often taken-for-granted processes and protocols. We can then also begin examining and planning the revisions we can implement to make strides toward our identified goals and equitable opportunities.

KEY TAKEAWAYS

Here's what to do to make the most of what we've covered in each section of this chapter.

Get Proximate

- Get close to those who are experiencing the inequity.
- Ask for insight from those closest to the inequity in authentic and meaningful ways.
- Use insight to make change.

Get Specific: Find Your Harbor

- Spend time reflecting on present inequities.
- Determine which inequities are personal, local, and immediate— meaning they are things within your locus of control.
- Decide on one to two equity goals (harbors).

Make Organizational Change

- Determine what top-down systems are in place.
- Apply an equity lens to the system: Who does this work for? Who does it not work for?
- Shift the system for equity.

2

SHARED EQUITY
Build a Coalition and Build Capacity

Race was invented to shut down solidarity and coalition building. Solidarity is subversive.

—Emma Dabiri

Building a coalition is an essential part of equity work. A *coalition* is a group of allies, like-minded individuals, peers, friends, family—you name it. Some members of your coalition will work alongside you in a school or district, while others may support you and your work in a personal capacity. The size of the coalition can be from a few individuals to a few hundred. A coalition is not necessarily a formal entity; it is instead those who are aligned with your equity direction and beliefs. Your coalition will support the work in whatever form that work takes. A coalition member can be in the trenches with you as a fellow educator or at the boardroom table as a professional ally. Coalition members' commitment to the work is more important than their positions or job titles. Engaging in the day-to-day grind of checking in, talking, and supporting is just as important as making big policy and budget decisions that impact the system. And as you build your coalition, don't forget to think about building capacity as well. When I say building capacity, I mean developing the skills and knowledge of individuals to speak to and lead this important work. This could look like listening to a lecture or panel together, cofacilitating a community meeting, or practicing how to react to and moderate difficult conversations. In short, you want to determine who your allies are and how can you learn together in order to make change.

While equity leadership will take on many forms, even the leader who is out front still needs allies for continuous learning and growth. I find myself often being the face of equity in my district, and it proves difficult. Being criticized in the media or seeing hate mail in your inbox day after day can be trying, no doubt. But it would be *impossible* if it were not for the coalition I have around me. Those on my immediate team, along with teachers, administrators, community members, and friends, help me stay optimistic and push me to know more. But even though we may find ourselves as the public face of equity, it is not about us. At the root of equity work is actively decentering oneself in order to amplify and increase opportunities for others. This can be a difficult balance, as leaders are chosen to be outspoken and give voice to their areas of expertise. But it is this decentering and critical self-awareness that serve as the foundations for achieving shared equity.

In this chapter, we will discuss how to embark on this necessary personal work before exploring the four parts to building a coalition: (1) who you will include in your coalition, (2) how you will offer multiple entry points (opportunities to engage in the work) to build your coalition, (3) how far to push, and (4) what you can focus on to build capacity.

HOW TO BECOME AN EFFECTIVE ALLY

Leaders at the school and district levels must consider how to use their own privilege to advance conversations and actions to best serve marginalized groups. Being a district leader or school leader means that you are already in a place of positional power, not including your race and gender. If you experience privilege due to your race or gender as well, this needs to be taken into consideration as you lead this work. A *White ally*, for example, is someone who is racially White and uses that racial privilege in order to elevate the voices of the oppressed and advance the causes that are central to historically marginalized communities. Further, there is much to consider even in the term *ally*, especially if you are part of a privileged group aiming to make conditions better for a marginalized group—so much so that many choose instead to be called *co-conspirators*. Allyship, in practice, has often come to mean effusive words but little action. Alicia Garza (as cited in Move to End Violence, 2016), cofounder of Black Lives Matter, describes the more action-oriented *co-conspiracy* as being:

> About what we do in action, not just in language. It is about moving through guilt and shame and recognizing that we did not create none of this stuff. And so what we are taking responsibility for is the power that we hold to transform our conditions.

Consider the following from antibias education organization Learning for Justice (2018), formerly Teaching Tolerance: "Being an effective ally requires significant self-reflection and a strong sense of self-identity. Any educator can become an ally, but the journey might look different depending on one's identity, experience and familiarity with issues of power and privilege."

One of the most helpful activities for reflecting on your identity is to complete an activity called *identity mapping*. The purpose of the activity is to become more aware of the different identities you hold, as well as think critically about which identities are generally seen (for example, race) and unseen (for example, religion). As you create and reflect on your own identity map, consider categories such as race, gender, class, ability, language, citizenship status, and more (you can access a thorough, step-by-step process for identity mapping at http://bit.ly/3fMfAMM). While being a cook or a dog lover can surely be important aspects of our identities, they are not likely to be the ones that show up when leading equity work. Identities like religion and citizenship status are not as outwardly visible to others but can weigh more heavily in the decisions and biases we have, meaning these identities manifest more as we embark on our equity journeys. Knowing all the aspects and intersections of your identity is a powerful tool in navigating your own privilege and allyship. For instance, if you are a citizen of the country you reside in, you have a certain amount of privilege that undocumented people do not. Being aware of this privilege (often, people do not even think about their citizenship status, which is a privilege in and of itself) means that you can more meaningfully navigate spaces and conversations as an ally to immigrants and refugees.

In figure 2.1, I've included an example of what my own identity map looks like.

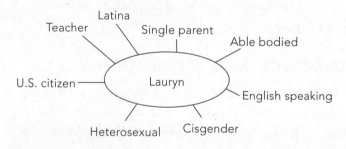

Figure 2.1: Identity map example.

*Visit **go.SolutionTree.com/diversityandequity** for a free reproducible version of this figure.*

As an example of being a true ally and not one in name only, I worked with middle school principal Tad Sherman, a big talker with a big personality, when he was about two years into his equity journey. He was aware of the positional and racial privilege afforded to him as a middle school principal and a White man. Tad was continually deepening his learning and knowledge as a White ally. He shared with me that in staff conversations, he had committed to being one of the last to talk—if he even talked at all. This was his way of elevating the voices of others, knowing that his narrative, with him being a straight White male, was already a dominant part of the decisions and conversation. Here is one small way Tad dedicated himself to listening more and speaking less. In conversations he was involved in, he ensured that women and people of color received more time to speak than him, and therefore their perspectives were included in the larger context. In turn, his discomfort with staying quiet (which was a struggle) helped him learn more about his staff and make his own perspective more robust.

Tad decentered himself by making sure his voice did not dominate conversation. This decentering of self is key to allyship. It involves a self-awareness that includes the ability to monitor inner thoughts and values (Eurich, 2018). Such self-awareness can take multiple forms and is important to note as we create a coalition for equity work. While you may not be in the exact position of the middle school principal, Tad, consider the following reflection questions as you partake in this work.

- Who is part of my coalition?
- Is my coalition composed of a diverse group of identities, or is it homogenous in its makeup?
- Does the coalition I am building challenge me and help me grow in my own equity journey?

Whether you have a sort of coalition you're taking stock of or you are entering into coalition building in equity work for the first time, the remainder of the chapter will help you build on these reflection questions as you aim to lead with a diverse, productive, high-quality team.

WHOM TO INCLUDE IN YOUR COALITION

First, let's identify who will support and learn alongside you. Which groups of people should you should focus on to build out your coalition? It helps to break the process of building a coalition down with a process called *power mapping*, which means mapping out possible coalition members on a bell curve or a similar visual representation of your team. Individuals in public positions like community organizers and policy makers use power mapping as a way to capitalize on sociology research theory and assess the sociopolitical context of their work (Noy, 2008). For the sake of this explanation, let's say you are a school equity leader looking to start or advance equity work. You have a large team of educators who are in multiple places on their individual equity journeys. Imagine a normal distribution bell curve—see figure 2.2 if, like me, you're a bit removed from high school mathematics. Using this curve as a guide, you can visually map where your colleagues are around you, identifying who will help, who can be convinced, and who you need to spend less energy on; in this way you can be intentional in your efforts to build a coalition. Let's say that half your team (group A) is on board with equity efforts, meaning those members will go with the flow and share a common vision with you. This may be 50 percent of your team, or it may be more or less.

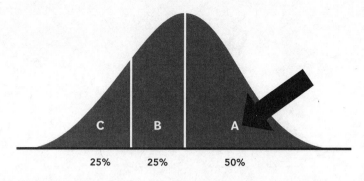

25%   25%   50%

Figure 2.2: Bell curve for building a coalition—focus on group A.

Those in group A may be self-starters in the area of equity or those who are passionate about equity and are ready to engage in other ways. These are the people who are already reading equity-related books on their own, attending weekend workshops, or working or teaching with a social justice lens. Group A is the group with whom you will be deepening equity learning capacity so that members can further lead efforts.

As you analyze your staff's readiness for this work, one thing to pay attention to is an unwanted *echo chamber effect*, which, according to GCFGlobal (n.d.), is when individuals are in an environment or context in which they encounter only information or opinions that reflect and reinforce their own. Equity-minded leaders often spend their time within one group (an echo chamber), which can lead to false assumptions about what the broader school community is ready for. While you map your own staff, think about who you are interacting with and what voices are most present in meetings and in the ongoing work at your site. In order to accurately gauge the readiness of your group, you will need to diversify your input, but remember to focus on engagement and interest rather than falling into assumptions about the identities of others.

Now, let's look at the other half of the bell curve, as shown in figure 2.3 (page 30). When looking to expand a coalition, we want to focus energy on group B.

These are the team members who are not necessarily excited about equity work but will listen to their peers' successes and will often hesitantly go along with new initiatives. These are the people who will need extra time and training but are not immovable. The tide of change and pedagogy will carry them along, but in the end, they are open to trying new and different things. They may be sarcastic or engage in parking-lot complaining, but these educators can rise to a challenge and will try new things. It is not an easy or quick shift, but this is the group you need to focus on.

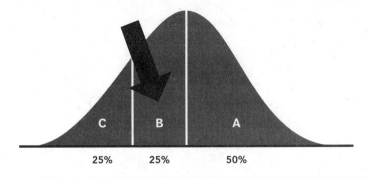

Figure 2.3: Bell curve for building a coalition—focus on group B.

Finally, we have group C, as shown in figure 2.4. This is the group of people who, for whatever reason, are completely against what you are trying to do. To be clear, group C will not and can not be part of your coalition.

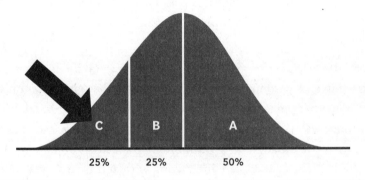

Figure 2.4: Bell curve for building a coalition—focus on group C.

I jokingly call this group *not your people*. I mean this with all respect to every individual in the education field, but also with the added emphasis that some people are not ready or willing in any way to make an effort to gain capacity for equity work or roll with the tide of change. We have all been a part of interpersonal workplace dynamics, and we are all likely familiar with how much time we spend on people who are the squeaky wheels and who bring negative energy into the workplace. We all know who they are—they have one foot out the door or are consumed by other events and things happening in their own lives. Further, team members in group C could be those stuck in past mindsets or unwilling to participate in their own growth as educators. They could be silent about equity-related discussions, or they could be outright hostile when the topic comes up.

This does not make them bad people or bad educators—it simply makes them not your people for this work. Now, do all students need to be treated equitably? Yes. But by spending our precious time and resources on a group that is stuck, we do not allow the group that is ripe for change (that is, group B) to be moved. The group C outliers need their own individual accountability from their supervisor and a plan that will ensure students and people in their area of influence are still being treated with the expectations of the school or office. Eventually, they will either learn to get on the ship or get off, so to speak. But in terms of direct equity work, it's best not to waste energy on them.

Here are three steps to determine your coalition.

1. Think about who all the people are on your team.

2. Consider where each of your team members fall (map out everyone) in each area of the coalition bell curve (group A, B, or C)? Spend some time on your own or with trusted team members to determine where the members of your team lie. There is no definite answer or exact test they will pass to end up in each area. This is also an ongoing and shifting answer—people and concepts are not monolithic, and there will be fluidity between groups based on timing and perceptions. The purpose of this is more to determine how difficult (or less difficult) your equity journey may be based on the team you have.

3. Now that you have your A, B, and C groups, you can start to look at strategies for your own unique situation. Is your A group large or small? Do you have a lot of naysayers or the opposite? Now that you have identified your B group, what would be some entry points that would match their personalities and unique strengths?

High School Example

What happens when your percentages look very different from the preceding bell curve models in figures 2.2 (page 29), 2.3, and 2.4? Or you have an administration that is not exactly on board with antiracist and equity work? One very small team of high school teachers created a grassroots movement that worked to build its own learning and capacity. The team members did not have administrative support, and it was a struggle for them to consider what the work of an equity team would look like in their very affluent and conservative area. They were timid about rocking the boat and were largely meeting outside school to have informal conversations.

While they were a small team, they were fiercely committed to their work, and the time they spent together was encouraging. Over the course of months, more and more equity champions made themselves known as word spread about what the team was doing. The small team of five grew to ten. While this is still a small number for a comprehensive high school staff, it shows that even a small team without support can grow—and that just by starting the work, you may empower others (who would otherwise be too scared) to join in. The team members still meet regularly in person or virtually to keep their conversation rolling. They still don't have the backing of administration, but they decided to take turns sending out articles and resources to staff via email in hopes that their voluntary coalition will continue to grow over time.

Tool

Have you seen the video of "Dancing Guy"? It is a funny, novel take on how leadership allows others to join in and it shows how, often, it is not the leader but the first follower who gives others permission to start a revolution. Visit https://youtu.be/fW8amMCVAJQ to watch the video. Consider showing it to a leadership team or in a training to make the point of how leaders are among us (and it always gets a good laugh, too).

Elementary School Example

An elementary school I worked with was eager to start an equity team and needed guidance about where to begin. The small team's members were despondent about the prospect of equity at their school and were fearful of backlash. I suggested we map their school staff first, using the coalition bell curve, to see the entirety of what we were looking at in terms of change.

The elementary school where this small team worked was enormous, with more than 120 staff members and multiple tracks of year-round calendars. As we broke down group C, the team soon realized that it consisted of only seven to ten people. We talked about how the number of people in this group was very small in comparison to the whole staff, but that the attention and energy it took to address its members and manage their outbursts had made it feel like group C was much larger. When the team members saw that such a small percentage of their staff was in group C, they were more prepared to identify who was in group B, where they knew they needed to focus.

After we finished mapping their staff, we determined group B included twenty-five individuals. The realization that about 70 percent of their staff were in groups A and B gave team members a whole new perspective on what the work would look like at their school. Their assumption that most of the school would be unwilling to engage in equity work proved false, and knowing the real numbers of staff to focus on helped them feel much more hopeful about their outcomes. Use the blank bell curve in figure 2.5 as you map your own team.

HOW TO USE MULTIPLE ENTRY POINTS TO BUILD YOUR COALITION

There is no single right way to enter into equity work. Think of your reason for taking this on. It could be a student, a training, a book you read, or an experience you had. As we bring others into equity work, we must recognize that there are also multiple entry points—certain activities or situations that spark their interest—for them

Instructions: Once you have taken some time to map your colleagues and work out who belongs to groups A, B, and C, determine roughly what percentages those groups represent. You can use the following bell curve template to indicate these percentages and label your groups. How much of your bell curve consists of group A? Group B? Group C?

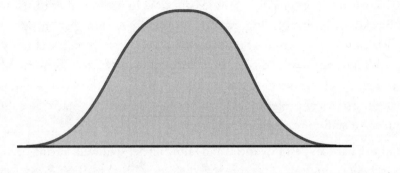

Figure 2.5: Bell curve for mapping a coalition.

*Visit **go.SolutionTree.com/diversityandequity** for a free reproducible version of this figure.*

as well. Some will shy away from a racial conversation but will talk about LGBTQ+ rights. Others will discuss poverty but not religion. While we recognize that many of these identities are intersectional in nature, people have comfort and pain points in terms of their level of ease engaging with each identity. Implicit biases and long-held cultural norms largely dictate what topics we will engage in. According to the Kirwan Institute for the Study of Race and Ethnicity (2012):

> The implicit associations we harbor in our subconscious cause us to have feelings and attitudes about other people based on characteristics such as race, ethnicity, age, and appearance. These associations develop over the course of a lifetime beginning at a very early age through exposure to direct and indirect messages.

Whatever subject ignites passion and brings people to the table is what we must leverage. Best practice is to show grace and to meet our students where they are, and the same must happen for adults. In the following sections, I go into detail about three possible entry points: (1) a large event, (2) a community push, and (3) explicit expectations. It's not a comprehensive list of entry points to equity work, but it does provide multiple contexts for how people can enter this important work.

Entry Point—Large Event

Sometimes, it takes a large and profound or disruptive event to create an avenue for equity. I think of the many people who have been called to action over police shootings of innocent Black Americans, or in response to national attention on board-ing school atrocities in Canada. These moments of reckoning with a racial past can spur movement and action for people. A colleague and friend of mine, an assistant principal named Charlesa, found herself in the middle of a media circus when she sent out an email about Black Lives Matter at School Week. This movement began in 2016, when a large group of Seattle educators joined together to affirm and sup-port Black lives in schools. It grew into a larger movement that encouraged schools and districts across the United States to join in a week of action in February each year. Charlesa knew her staff had been involved with equity work for some time, so she sent out an email encouraging staff to learn more about the week of action and par-ticipate in a series of professional learnings that would take place. She also attached resources for staff to read about.

Despite Charlesa's best intentions and knowing her staff well, having been a member of the school community for more than ten years, this email triggered a small group at her school, which then alerted local media. It blew up in the news locally, and as a Black female administrator, Charlesa was left in an unfortunate position in which she had to defend herself for encouraging others to engage with a Black Lives Matter at School Week campaign. She had to grapple with her actions and the actions of others while under intense scrutiny.

Her principal was a White man who believed strongly that Charlesa had done noth-ing wrong and that the actions of a few were not representative of the entire staff. He communicated to her that he would address the uproar with the staff. At the next staff meeting, the principal led an honest and, quite frankly, very bold conversation about what values their school stood for and what they believed in as educators. The administration team was seen as a united front, and detractors or those who did not agree with the values of the school were encouraged to find another school that better suited their beliefs. Now, even though this was a brave and very tense conversation, it showed how the principal used his privilege to support Charlesa, who in turn was able to further identify who they should focus their time and training on (and who, perhaps, were *not their people* and belonged in group C). Further, this event led many equity champions at Charlesa's school to come forward. The tide of equity shifted, and her coalition became even clearer; she now leads one of the longest-running and most successful teams in the district.

Entry Point—Community Push

Another entry point is to use a *community push*: tried-and-true measures like food and coffee to ease the conversation with the school community. Some of the most suc-cessful schools I have worked with used a coffee-and-conversations model to create an open and welcoming space to discuss difficult topics. The participants weren't asked to do any sort of homework or prework, and schools would advertise the topics and dates well ahead of time so team members could decide whether their schedule allowed them to attend. The group might watch a TED Talk together and then discuss it or read an article and then break into groups. The processes for conversing remained undemanding so that the content could stay rich, like in a classroom. The important aspect of this entry point is that it allows peers to socialize while discussing the idea of equity and to normalize equity conversations in a school setting. When the entry point is not driven by administration but rather by the team itself, it can be—and often is—more influential among team members.

Entry Point—Explicit Expectations

Lastly, some members may arrive at equity work through explicit expectations. These are simply tasks or processes that you encourage or require to help staff practice equity work. Let's say that as an equity leader, you decide that you want all staff to engage in greeting students at the door as they come into class as a core practice. Whether you are the administration or a leader of a site equity team, you understand the why for this practice. A study conducted by professor of educational psychology Clayton R. Cook and colleagues (2018) shows that the simple act of meeting students at the classroom door and personally greeting each one can increase classroom engagement by 20 percent. You convey this information to your staff and then share your expectation for personal greetings with them. You get some grumblings from the staff, mostly from groups B and C in your bell curve. As time goes on, and as you monitor your expectation, a few of your grumbling teachers begin to come around. They see that their fellow educators are all complying with this expectation, and, more important, they enjoy greeting the students. They even share with their colleagues that they see the difference it has made and that they will continue with the practice.

Whether it is a major event, a community push, or an explicit expectation, varied ways to engage with equity are critical. And there are many other opportunities that brilliant school and district leaders have created and that you will find, too. The more opportunities we identify or offer, the more likely we are to build our coalition.

HOW FAR TO PUSH

Now that we have identified which groups we should focus on and how we might identify or design their entry points, we can talk about how far to push when we do this work. For gauging how much we can ask of our coalition, I am a firm believer in the work of leadership experts Ronald Heifetz, Alexander Grashow, and Marty Linsky (2009) and their book, *The Practice of Adaptive Leadership*. Organizations all over the world have used and benefited from their groundbreaking theory on the zone of disequilibrium.

For the purposes of their work, Heifetz and his colleagues (2009) describe *disequi-librium* as the "period of disturbance" in which people experiment with solutions (p. 28). I often refer to it as the anxiety and stress that a person or team is feeling. The foundational research of psychologists Jean Piaget and Bärbel Inhelder (1969) indi-cates that for us to learn, the mind must enter a state of disequilibrium whereupon it encounters new information and has to develop or modify new or existing *schema* (self-knowledge about objects, places, or people). Piaget and Inhelder's (1969) theory of schema has been extended beyond reading comprehension to include how cultural knowledge impacts overall literacy development and practice (McVee, Dunsmore, & Gavelek, 2005). That is, we must be uncomfortable in order to learn. Like our stu-dents, who we push out of their comfort zones as we introduce new skills and concepts, we adults must also be pushed. There is a place that is productive for us, where we cross this threshold of change. This is the *productive zone*. We are just uncomfortable enough to learn but not uncomfortable enough that we meet our *limit of tolerance*. The *limit of tolerance* is when we reach "work avoidance" (Heifetz et al., 2009, p. 30). In equity work, the limit of tolerance is when we start to lose people. Keeping people in the productive zone, shown in figure 2.6, is a delicate balance. Over time, the amount of disequilibrium people are able to tolerate increases. The arrows show the balance of pushing people into the productive zone, but also being able to apply structure and routine in order to make sure they do not reach work avoidance.

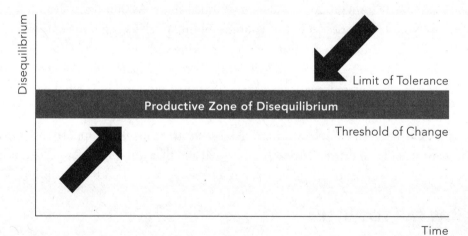

Source: Adapted from Heifetz et al., 2009.

Figure 2.6: Productive zone of disequilibrium.

My former boss and mentor Rodney Trice, chief equity officer at the school dis-trict in Chapel Hill, North Carolina, often compares the zone of disequilibrium to getting food perfectly cooked in the kitchen: we turn up the heat in order to push people into their productive zone, and then we turn down the heat right before, or when, they reach their limit of tolerance.

We can approach this zone of disequilibrium theory through a different and more specific version that fits our context as equity leaders. Let's take a look at an example. A local parent-teacher association (PTA) group we have is dedicated to conversations around race and bias. Its members are at the forefront of leading parents and the school community they serve in confronting the impact of gentrification and magnet schools (public schools that offer special programs or curriculum in order to attract a more diverse population) influence on their small urban elementary school. They pushed the productive zone of disequilibrium for parents who attended PTA meetings. It was not normal PTA fundraising and business when families showed up—but learning and growing were happening! Attendees were having conversations and parents were engaging with their children about the history of integration and race in schools. Then the PTA offered an article on White privilege. The disequilibrium shot through the zone of productivity and past the limit of tolerance. Parents didn't show up for the related meeting, and it ended up making national news. Angry phone calls and media coverage followed, and the PTA had to turn the heat completely off.

In my opinion, the PTA members were undoubtedly courageous in their efforts and were intentional about the work they wanted to do. However, they had misidentified the productive zone of families. The PTA board had believed it to be much higher than it was. The group learned very quickly, and quite painfully, from pushback that while the school community was ready to talk about race, community members weren't ready to talk about White privilege. The PTA suffered and equity work halted completely. Work avoidance turned into work stoppage and equity discussions took a few years to gain traction again.

After reflection, this PTA and school equity team realized that they had not spent enough time helping to equip the community with baseline knowledge of the word privilege and establishing norms for engagement and communication with each other for these types of conversations. Additionally, the team members learned that the community of parents had not spent enough time gaining trust with one another in order to talk about *their own* privilege in that space. This team, its journey to do what is best for its community, and a misstep in identifying that community's limit of tolerance give us one example of the delicate balance of push and pull involved in equity work.

WHAT TO FOCUS ON TO BUILD CAPACITY

So you have your coalition. You know who is in group A and who you need to focus efforts on in group B. It's important to note that the size of this coalition is not as important as the passion of those in it. Each bell curve will look completely different, depending on any number of factors, including your unique geography, sociopolitical contexts, and school environment. Maybe you are heavier in group C and lighter in groups A and B. Keep pushing. You *will* find the right people to head to your harbor with.

The next step to building a coalition is to determine what you will collectively learn to deepen the knowledge and capacity of the group. This learning should align with what you determined to be your equity goal or harbor. One of my favorite ways to zero in on a plan is to go through a visioning protocol with the team. The School Reform Initiative (SRI) has a wide bank of such protocols to help teams identify their learning focus, or you can use some of your tried-and-true strategies like consensus models or surveys. One especially useful protocol from SRI is named Back to the Future and offers a structure for teams to present ideas in a poster format without them being formalized; then the team refines the goals through clarifying and specific questions (August, 2008).

Tool

School Reform Initiative has a vast, searchable database of protocols and advisories. Visit www.schoolreforminitiative.org to find the tool that best fits your site and circumstances.

The ultimate result of such a protocol should be what learning your team needs in order to achieve your shared goal and best serve your stakeholders. For example, if your team's goal is to increase family engagement at school events, you may look to cultural events or community partners to learn from. If your goal is staff knowledge and awareness of instructional bias, what book or video could you access together that will make sure you are all on the same page? The idea is to have a common learning experience so that members of the team speak the same language on equity. This way, you all have common ground to refer to when having conversations and making further plans. Additionally, just as we use anchor texts for students, anchor texts can be helpful as a reference point again and again with adults—and they don't always have to be traditional, or written, texts. See table 2.1 for a few examples of shared learning in action.

As you create your own shared learning to develop your coalition's capacity, you'll want to keep the following considerations in mind.

- Does your proposal center the intended beneficiary in the conversation? (For example, if your school harbor is about improving student outcomes, does the book you are reading cover instructional strategies for improving student outcomes or is it just the latest "it" book?)

- What is the shared learning or professional development in the school or district? Does it cover equity? Is there space for equity-based learning?

- What equity-centered courses or trainings occur in the district or locally?

- Are there EdCamps (free, public events where the participants determine the sessions and topics; https://digitalpromise.org/edcamp) and other grassroots organizations that you can connect with?

Table 2.1: Examples of Shared Learning in Action

Group	Learning Focus	Shared Learning
Teachers	Culturally responsive pedagogy	In-depth cohort book study of Zaretta Hammond's (2015) *Culturally Responsive Teaching and the Brain*
PTA	Connection with families	Family dinner night at a local food market, where everyone is on neutral territory and teachers and staff can come and eat with families. Prompts written in multiple languages can appear on the tables for families to learn more about each other (for example: What does your student like best in school? What are some of your family traditions?)
Equity team	Discipline disproportionality	Group viewing of *Pushout: The Criminalization of Black Girls in Schools*, a film by Monique W. Morris and Jacoba Atlas (Carney, Atlas, & Morris, 2019), with conversation afterward at a local Black-owned restaurant
District staff	Socialization of equity concepts so that there is a shared language and foundational understanding of commonly misunderstood phrases such as antiracist or LGBTQ+	Lunch-and-learn event, with a diverse assortment of guest speakers who will speak to the definitions and foundational knowledge of each concept; staff members bringing their own lunches at a central district office site

As I stated at the beginning of the chapter, your coalition is an essential component to leading equity work. Building a coalition and working to build the equity capacity of all involved is how you create a shift in the culture of your school or district. These *are* your people. And your coalition will form a community that offers the inspiration and accountability you all need as your collective equity journey continues. This process of working and learning together will offer opportunities to share in equity leadership and in responsibilities for facilitating the work. The coalition can share many responsibilities: holding meetings, offering discussion prompts, choosing materials, facilitating professional development, and much more. Through this collective approach, the work belongs to *us* instead of *me*.

In an effort to streamline the shared learning process, consider the reflection questions, either alone or with your coalition, in figure 2.8. Our equity goal guides us to what learning we need to do to reach said goal. After you know what learning the team members or staff need, then you can research and ask for suggestions for what the text or experience will be. Often, we jump right to meeting times and dates and buying things—but I urge you to leave the logistics for last. Those details will fall in place once you decide on the big equity goals and learning texts.

Reflection Question	Response
What is our equity goal?	
What do we need to learn or understand in order to do this work?	
What shared text or experience will best help us learn what we need to reach our goal?	
What are the logistics for our shared learning (time, place, facilitator, and so forth)?	

Figure 2.8: Reflection questions for better understanding an equity goal.

*Visit **go.SolutionTree.com/diversityandequity** for a free reproducible version of this figure.*

Getting specific—finding your harbor—is the first step to then working backward to determine the next steps.

CONCLUSION

In this chapter, we learned first what it means to be an effective ally when it comes to equity work: how leaders may use their positional power to facilitate dialogue and action that will benefit marginalized groups, and how we all must consider our own identities as we undertake this work. We've learned who to include in our coalition and how to expand that coalition, giving a special focus to those who, though perhaps hesitant and in need of an extra push, are open to new directions and new initiatives. We've explored the ways we can leverage people's individual whys for entering into equity work and how we can ignite learning among our coalition with just the right amount of disequilibrium. Finally, we looked at how we may create common learning experiences among our coalition members so that we're all speaking the same language as we proceed with our collective work.

KEY TAKEAWAYS

Here's what to do to make the most of what we've covered in each section of this chapter.

How to Become an Effective Ally

- Consider how to use your own privilege, whether it's the privilege of positional power, race, gender, or all three, to support and amplify the voices of marginalized groups.

- Complete an identity map to help you reflect on your own visible and invisible identities.

Whom to Include in Your Coalition

- Map your staff for groups A, B, and C.

- Consider who is in your group A in order to build your coalition and help you create goals and plans.

How to Use Multiple Entry Points to Build Your Coalition

- Provide a diverse array of opportunities for staff to engage with to increase the number of opportunities to enter into equity work.

- Diversify topics and opportunities to discuss and engage.

- Meet adults where they are, just as you do with students.

How Far to Push

- Determine how you will identify disequilibrium.

- Name what you think your team's limit of tolerance could be.

- Develop strategies for turning up the heat and turning down the heat.

What to Focus on to Build Capacity

- Tie shared learning to your equity focus or harbor.

- Determine shared texts or media.

- Share equity leadership and facilitation responsibilities with staff members who have built up their learning and capacity.

3

STRUCTURED EQUITY
Work the System

It's not enough to change the system.
We need to change ourselves.

—Assata Shakur

So far, we have covered how to analyze top-down systems in order to create change as well as how to build an equity-minded coalition. In this chapter, we focus on how the system within which we operate—whether a school or district—upholds inequities by the very nature of its existence. Structured equity is about how we concentrate on making equity shifts in process and goals to the teams and groups that are already in place.

Ever hear the phrase "Every system is perfectly designed to get the results it gets"? Schools and districts have been intentionally designed through generations of laws and mandates for the student outcomes we are seeing. Further, we as a society have become very comfortable with the outcomes we are seeing. The well-known narrative that marginalized students do not perform as well academically as their more privileged counterparts (National Assessment of Educational Progress, n.d.) is well known *because* of society's relative comfort with or tolerance of this imbalance. Education researcher Lisa Delpit (2012), tells us:

> There is no "achievement gap" at birth. . . . If we do not recognize the brilliance before us, we cannot help but carry on the stereotypic societal views that these children are somehow damaged goods and that they cannot be expected to succeed. (p. 5)

The teams and people we have put in place as stewards of these systems are the decision makers who carry out the designs that then perpetuate our societal inequalities. I urge you to consider how the teams and formally arranged spaces (staff meetings, committees, and the like) you already have in place are contributing to the student outcomes you are getting. This means looking critically at who is making the decisions as well as what topics are key areas of focus.

The importance of critically analyzing who is making decisions was made even more clear to me during one particular meeting I was in about social-emotional learning. There were representatives from across the state there to talk about how to create goals and a vision for a larger district plan. A woman insisted that we "invite marginalized groups to the table." I know her heart was in the right place when she said this, but intent does not equal impact, and every time I hear this metaphor, it rubs me the wrong way. This statement assumes that the status quo is the host and keeper of the table and that they have the power to invite *others*.

Shirley Chisholm (as cited by the Edward M. Kennedy Institute, 2021), educator, author, and the first Black woman elected to the U.S. Congress, famously said, "If they don't give you a seat at the table, bring a folding chair." This mentality of marginalized and historically oppressed people having to make room for themselves at the decision-making table, or the idea that they must wait to be invited, is a symbolic example of race and power dynamics. For instance, power dynamics in school systems could mean that a team or department decides what steps to implement to increase the academic success of Black male students—without ever talking to Black male students. People who have not historically held power should be the decision makers for what most closely affects them. Their voices and expertise are what the status quo needs to seek out. Marginalized people are not party guests, and when a biased system has excluded them from the decision-making process, we people in power should instead hope to be invited to *their* table. Indeed, we cannot make decisions for those closest to the inequity. So how do we restructure the party host–party guest dynamic?

In this chapter, we will discuss how to use the teams you *already have* in order to create change and shift the mindset and goals of a team. Earlier, we discussed how equity teams are not the key to achieving equity—they are a piece of the work, not the entirety of it. To achieve systemic equity, we must move into an intentionally inclusive approach where all teams within a school or district are equity centered in goals and actions.

Figure 3.1 offers a visual example of what this shift to being equity centered would look like. The traditional structure of how teams work within a school includes various teams working toward their own goals. These teams dip into the area covered

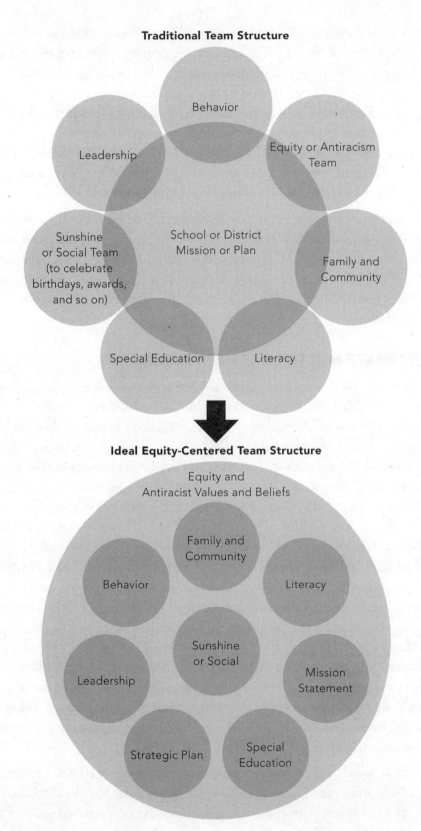

Traditional Team Structure

Behavior

Leadership

Equity or Antiracism Team

Sunshine or Social Team (to celebrate birthdays, awards, and so on)

School or District Mission or Plan

Family and Community

Special Education

Literacy

Ideal Equity-Centered Team Structure

Equity and Antiracist Values and Beliefs

Family and Community

Behavior

Literacy

Leadership

Sunshine or Social

Mission Statement

Strategic Plan

Special Education

Figure 3.1: Equity shifts in school and district team structures.

by the school or district plan and may overlap with one another, but generally, they operate independently. In this traditional structure, equity work is treated and seen as an independent concept—just another spoke on the wheel. In the equity-centered model, on the other hand, equity moves from being one spoke on the wheel to *being* the wheel. All the teams come together and operate according to equity and antiracist values and beliefs (represented by the larger circle on the right). Each team has stakeholders, norms, processes, and goals that reflect the school's or district's values and beliefs. This shift with our teams and formally arranged spaces is another way that equity becomes the very fabric of our school or district.

While equity teams are a great idea, we know that education is already team heavy. The idea is not to reinvent the wheel or add more teams to already full plates but to make the teams and formally arranged spaces you already have in place work differently. We will look at how to incorporate multiple stakeholders and their perspectives into the team goal and how to shift the team's goals and processes to be more equity centered in nature.

INCORPORATE MULTIPLE STAKEHOLDERS

Stakeholders are those who have a vested interest in the success and growth of your school or district. They are students and staff, but they are also community members and families. We must widen our definition of stakeholders to include those who are less recognized but are working hard in their positions. In many situations, valuable voices, like those of receptionists, assistants, and people in other support positions, can go overlooked. For example, let me tell you about the greatest front-office receptionist I have ever seen, Ms. Moore. She greeted each person who walked in the door with such genuine love and attention that I found myself *wanting* to go to the front office for meetings just so I could see her. I witnessed her giving hugs, laughing and joking with staff, and being a quick resource of information for families as they came in. One time, I saw her greet a new student and her mother, who was enrolling her daughter at the school. The mother explained that it would be her third school that year and that her daughter was shy after having moved from another state. Ms. Moore kept smiling at the young girl, and finally she looked her right in the eye and said, "This is where you are supposed to be. This is the best school in the world, and it's even better now because you'll be here." The girl was grinning so big by the time she left she was almost skipping to her car in anticipation of her new school. The genuine care Ms. Moore had for her school, a new student, and all who crossed her path was something truly remarkable.

As we create teams at our school, a staff member in a position such as a receptionist, like Ms. Moore, would more than likely be overlooked. She is a Black woman working at a majority White and Asian school. She is not a certified teacher, and many see her sphere of influence as solely the front desk. But consider the power of having someone like Ms. Moore on a team. Her voice, perspective, and knowledge of the school community are priceless! There are individuals like Ms. Moore everywhere: cafeteria workers, school bus drivers, crossing guards, instructional aides, and more. Again, we must widen our definition of *stakeholder* to include those who are less recognized but are working just as hard. Some of our stakeholders are lateral in the sense that they are fighting and doing the same work as us; neighboring districts, schools, and organizations might have important input for us to consider. Figure 3.2 offers some reflection questions to consider as you identify stakeholders.

Reflection Question	Response
Who are the stakeholders at our site?	
What voices do we lack in our teams? What voices need to be elevated and amplified?	
Are certified and noncertified staff voices included at the same level of participation?	
Are the stakeholders diverse and representative of the school population?	
What barriers may exist to stakeholder engagement?	
Who are lateral stakeholders we can access, such as other schools and districts?	
Who are the community members and organizations working for education?	
What is the capacity and representation of the parent-teacher group?	

Figure 3.2: Reflection questions for identifying stakeholders.

*Visit **go.SolutionTree.com/diversityandequity** for a free reproducible version of this figure.*

These reflection questions will help you to apply a critical lens to your teams and ensure that they are diverse and representative of the community you serve. And the representation gap between students and educators is large: according to the

U.S. Department of Education (2019), almost 80 percent of educators in the United States are White despite only 52 percent of students identifying as White. The same gap appears in other countries as well; in the United Kingdom, for example, over 85 percent of teachers and 65 percent of their students identify as White British (Department for Education, 2021a, 2021b). As we talk about stakeholders, it is critical that we also discuss how race and identity show up in decision-making spaces. The party host–party guest dynamic is exacerbated by this racial divide in our schools and districts. Those who hold decision-making power are overwhelmingly White even in demographics that are not majority White. Research from the United States, Canada, and the United Kingdom shows that the percentage of BIPOC educators is continuing to fall farther behind the percentage of BIPOC students (Ryan, Pollock, & Antonelli). Additionally, this cultural hierarchy that students observe in schools and elsewhere sends the message that White people are better equipped and more deserving of decision-making roles. Taking all this into consideration, we as equity leaders must demand an increase in access for marginalized groups. As I've said, asking for marginalized voices to come to the table further reinforces the status quo. Instead, teams need to shift from inviting them to the table to going to where they are, similar to my colleagues who've implemented home visits, as I will explain a bit later in this chapter.

Another example of going to where marginalized voices are is bridging the divide between district office personnel and site-based personnel with an initiative to become more proximate. For instance, my mom, who has been in school-leadership positions for more than twenty years, shared with me that one of the school districts where she worked implemented a policy assigning each district staff member at the director level or above to a school site in the district. The expectation was for these staff members to adopt a classroom and visit once a week. They could play at recess, read to students, and offer general help during activities and transitions. Whatever their task was, it was secondary to the goal of becoming more connected to the day-to-day life of the school. This policy took place in a diverse district, predominately Latino/a and Black, with a high Title I population. The district office staff, on the other hand, is largely White and affluent.

As a principal, my mom appreciated the extra hands on deck but more so the relationships that developed between the district office and the various sites where the district staff built relationships. By meeting on a common playing field, the district office and site-based stakeholders were able to interact and talk in an authentic way—where the power dynamics shifted to place district office staff as listeners and contributors. Furthermore, decentering their own Whiteness and positional authority was essential to the district office staff listening and supporting from a learner lens.

Many of the district staff people who participated in this policy had been out of schools for a long time, or perhaps had never been teachers (as is the case with many district departments that are service or facility focused). My mom laughed while telling me about it, noting that some of the brave ones even planned lessons and brought in ideas from their own work to make connections to the units the students were studying. This ongoing interaction helped district staff members see the daily inequities brought on by limited resources and the struggles of students learning English and served as a much-needed wake-up call to their priorities when they went back to the district office each day. Consider the many ways in which the values of getting proximate (from chapter 1, page 11) and incorporating diverse stakeholders can benefit your school or district.

SHIFT TEAM GOALS AND PROCESSES

After identifying who our stakeholders are and where they come from, we can more accurately gauge the teams we want to target in making equity shifts. *Equity shifts* are small but mighty changes in how we conduct business on teams, committees, and other formal staff groupings. Ideally, we would make equity shifts in all our teams, both school and district. However, for process's sake, we must focus on one or a few teams at a time. This more concentrated focus means we avoid growing too fast and risking the fidelity and authenticity with which we are making changes. For instance, if you have identified that your stakeholders are predominately students and families who are learning English, then you may want to pay special attention to equity shifts that can occur in English-learner or family- and community-engagement committees.

Further, shifting systems to be more equitable is inherently about them being more *open*. Increasing access and opening up a system for valuable input, dialogue, and collective action stem from the theory that healthy organizations benefit from continuous interaction with their environment. The following list includes examples, at all levels, of open and closed systems in education.

My brother, Landon Mascareñaz (the *other* Dr. Mascareñaz), is a leader in family and community engagement in the education sphere. He writes extensively about open systems, and in the following list, I've included some of his cut-and-dried examples of what this looks like (and doesn't look like) to show the close relationship between *systems theory* (the perception of organizations as extended social systems that must interconnect with the world around them) and equity work (Mascareñaz, 2017).

- **Open:** A teacher goes on a home visit, opening up the physical walls of the classroom to include parents' perspectives.

- **Closed:** Over the course of the year, a teacher creates a ten-minute window on one day to speak to a parent.

- **Open:** A school creates an opportunity for parents to explore the academic standards all students must meet, perhaps by providing access to physical or electronic copies of each grade level's essential standards, opening up the learning environment for parent involvement.

- **Closed:** A school hosts a back-to-school night using only English-language materials and presentations, when more than half the parents speak another language.

- **Open:** A school undergoes a community-driven turnaround process, meaning the school and district have opened up design and creation of curriculum to parents and families.

- **Closed:** A school loses enrollment, experiences academic decline, and refuses to take feedback from families about why.

- **Open:** A district creates opportunities for meaningful feedback loops and even decision making with parents and caregivers, opening up its resources and power for true co-creation of learning.

- **Closed:** A district makes a major decision without any input from families, communities, or other stakeholders.

By another name, equity shifts are moves to open systems. They facilitate access and transparency so that all stakeholders are able to reach their highest potential within the system. Let's look at some examples from elementary, middle, and high school, after which we'll cover how these shifts look in action.

Elementary Example

Meeting the needs of families who are learning English is a common struggle for educators. According to the National Center for Education Statistics (2020), as of 2017, more than five million students in the U.S. school system were English learners, which comes out to be about 10 percent of U.S. students. An elementary school I worked with identified building a stronger family and community partnership as its equity goal. About 50 percent of the school's families were learning English, and it was seeing low turnout to school-sponsored events and a lack of responsivity to school communication. Now, this is a prime example of how the principal and the staff could have approached the issue with a deficit lens, such as declaring, "Well, those families don't value education," and then focusing their efforts elsewhere. However, using an equity lens, the principal started to think outside the box about what her families and community were dealing with and instead approached the issue by asking her staff how they could reach families in a more inclusive and holistic way. Her concern was that a translated newsletter was not sufficient; rather, in order to live out their school's equity goal, their team needed families and community members in the school as much as possible.

The school reached out to one of our brilliant family- and community-engagement coordinators from the district to determine next steps. The coordinator and the school decided as a team that in order to find out why families weren't showing up, they had to ask the families themselves. The school began training staff for home visits—they took translators and social workers with them on home visits, and together they gathered input about their school from their most important stakeholders. The feedback from families was twofold. First, they overwhelmingly loved the home visits. Students were so excited to see staff in their homes, and many of the families appreciated the translation services so that they could talk freely. Second, many families shared that while they were very involved in their children's education, it was difficult to come to school after hours because of transportation issues. Because of district neighborhood assignments, many of the families lived a thirty-minute drive from the campus, and many were without reliable transportation.

With this knowledge, the staff were able to make headway on their equity goal and gain perspective about how best to partner with their families moving forward. The staff continued their home visits, expanding the training to include a wider sample of teachers and instructional assistants. The staff also listened to families about how much they were struggling with speaking English and trying to find jobs to support their families. The principal, along with a team of staff members, applied for and won a grant in order to fund a family resource center that offered computers, English-language classes, and job-application support for anyone who came.

Tool

The Parent Teacher Home Visit Project is an outstanding resource for materials, training, and best practices around home visits. Visit www.pthvp.org to access these helpful materials.

This elementary school went deep into its training and practices to meet its families where they were. What's more, it experienced a meaningful shift in the way it interacted with families. The equity team members were prepared to operate as usual—to coordinate events and invite families to them—but their equity shift occurred when they went *to* the families instead. This is a prime example of how we avoid the party host–party guest mentality I addressed earlier. Further, we must keep in mind that family engagement and family involvement are two very different things. Family *engagement* is simply how a school creates opportunities for families to engage with school events or functions, while family *involvement* encompasses all the hundreds of things a family does to support and help its child or children thrive.

When educators say, "Those families just aren't involved" or "They just don't value education," I see educators who are using their own cultures and identities as a guide to what they consider to be involved, supportive family members. Consider the involvement it takes to house, clothe, feed, love, and support a child. As a single parent, I can attest that the amount of effort and involvement it takes just to get my kid to the school door each day is significant. I am extremely involved in my child's life. However, there have been many events I have missed at school for different reasons. It may have been because it was a daytime event and I was working or because I didn't have the childcare necessary to attend a parents-only function at night. Yet whatever the reasons were for my missing the event, *not valuing education* was certainly not one of them. I firmly believe that we would be hard-pressed to find a family who didn't care about its child's education.

Middle School Example

Jennifer Pride, a phenomenal educator and equity leader, is a middle school English teacher. She is a co-leader on her school's equity team and is one of the few Black educators at her school. Jennifer regularly held space for students during a scheduled elective period during their day. The elective period allowed students to go to a special elective class, play sports, or spend time in a teacher's room. Jennifer had a large group of BIPOC students who came to her class. The students were interested in reading something together, and they eventually covered titles like Nic Stone's (2017) *Dear Martin* and Angie Thomas's (2017) *The Hate U Give*. The space served an academic and social need for students but over time became an emotionally and mentally safe space for students who were not feeling safe elsewhere in the school.

As the students began to build a community together, Jennifer made a video of her students talking about what it felt like to be them at the school. She asked her students, "What do you need? What is missing? If you could talk to the staff, what would you like to say?" The videos were powerful, showing students being transparent and emotional as they described what it was like to "be me" at school. Jennifer shared them with the principal. They had long conversations about how best to show staff the videos and how to scaffold the conversations so that staff would feel reflective rather than blamed or shamed. The experience of watching the students speak became a catalyst for staff to begin a schoolwide book study on Zaretta Hammond's (2015) *Culturally Responsive Teaching and the Brain*. Through intentionally creating space for her students and encouraging their voices, Jennifer took an elective period and shifted it to create a powerful, supportive community for students and helped amplify their voices schoolwide.

High School Example

The leadership team at a high school met regularly to go over discipline data. It reviewed suspensions, talked about student behavior interventions, and discussed re-entry plans for students who had spent time out of school. Though the team met regularly to discuss what was going on, there was little movement in terms of reducing overall suspensions or their racial disproportionality rate. Team members communicated that they felt caught between trying to lower numbers to "keep the district happy" and removing students from class to show support for the teacher.

While disciplinary practices in schools are worthy of an in-depth conversation that takes into account the many possible equity angles, the purpose of this example is to show how the administration team in question took one of its tasks and began to apply an equity lens to it.

Tool

The book *Culturally Proficient Coaching: Supporting Educators to Create Equitable Schools* by Delores B. Lindsey, Randall B. Lindsey, and Richard S. Martinez (2006) is a great way to learn how to reinforce in-depth conversations and account for equity considerations.

The principal was looking for a way to make the issue of suspensions hit hard when presented. The team decided to break down disciplined students' time out of class into minutes in order to show the growing amount of instructional time those students missed when they were removed from the classroom. The principal knew that the sheer number of minutes would be starker and more resonant for her staff than a measurement of, say, two days. The instructional time lost became a running tally, and the connection between lost instruction and academic proficiency was evident. In sum, the administration team was already reviewing discipline data, but shifted its task to highlight the growing inequity of students' access to instructional time. This shift created a ripple effect at the school that called for brainstorming alternatives to suspension and increased teacher support for learning about culturally responsive engagement strategies. Utilizing culturally responsive strategies, as Ladson-Billings (1995) explains in her seminal work "Toward a Theory of Culturally Relevant Pedagogy," "not only addresses student achievement but also helps students to accept and affirm their cultural identity while developing critical perspectives that challenge inequities that schools (and other institutions) perpetuate" (p. 469). The staff engaged in professional development around Ladson-Billings's (1995) culturally responsive framework in order to have a deeper understanding of how their students were showing up to class and how their own culture dictated their responses to students.

Consider your own agenda for the team. How could you incorporate equity or your identified antiracist goals into the agenda so that they are visible and tangible to the entire team? For instance, list out the norms for courageous conversations at the top of the paper, or assign one team member the role within the group to ask, "Who does this decision work for? Who does it not work for?"

Tool

The New Team Habits is a helpful guide to creating new processes and procedures as a team. The authors created a method known as spark, expand, practice, apply, debrief (SEPAD) that is highly useful and walks through the process of incorporating new practices into team habits. Visit www.newteamhabits.com to access this guide.

Equity Shifts in Action

Actually putting equity shifts into action may feel challenging. The best place to start is by looking around you and identifying those places where these shifts are possible. Table 3.1 identifies school teams and the common processes and actions that each team works for. For each team and common process or action, an in-kind sample equity shift is provided.

Table 3.1: School Team Equity Shifts

School Teams and Formally Arranged Groups		
How can team processes or actions shift to include equity?		
School-Level Team	**Process or Actions**	**Equity-Shift Example**
Leadership	Co-created team norms	Include norms for how to have difficult conversations about race.
Professional learning team or grade-level team	Data talks	Analyze subgroups of historically marginalized students when having data conversations to highlight overall trends in representation and proportionality.
Social or sunshine	Decorating and gathering for Judeo-Christian holidays	Poll students and families about their most important cultural events and holidays; include these other celebrations in the school calendar, and use them as opportunities to learn about diverse cultures.
Behavior or discipline	Review referral data	Audit suspension and referral data for inconsistencies among racial groups; determine proportionality to school population.

In the leadership example, the equity shift occurs when co-created team norms go one step further to include norms for critical conversations about race. I want to expand on this example because the capacity of staff to engage in critical conversations with comfort is paramount to being able to move the pendulum of equity work. That is, how do we make change for marginalized groups if we can't even talk about those groups? Further, the ability to have these conversations can apply to virtually every educator space. Leadership teams often work to co-create a space for the norms that all team members adhere and agree to, and the equity shift comes into play when they ask, "How will our collective norms incorporate ways we talk about race and other difficult topics?" These norms may exist in the equity or diversity team, but integrating them into leadership teams ensures that both teams are now operating with race- and equity-centered norms.

Table 3.2 has equity-shift examples for some common district office teams. Again, these examples are not exhaustive but rather meant to provide you with ideas for how you can help the teams you *already have* progress toward shared equity goals.

Table 3.2: District Team Equity Shift

District Teams and Formally Arranged Spaces		
How can team processes or actions shift to include equity?		
District-Level Team	**Processes or Actions**	**Equity-Shift Example**
Academic achievement and advancement	Choose curriculum	Involve parents, students, and teachers in curriculum decisions and piloting programs.
Security	Train school resource officers in procedures	Require ongoing and systemic antibias and antiracist training.
Family and community engagement	Hold band concerts, awards ceremonies, or performances at district office or schools	Hold events at local libraries, recreation centers, and places of worship that are central to student and family neighborhoods.
Board of education	Public comment time	Include dedicated time slots for students and actively advertise for the board meeting to student groups that include historically marginalized individuals, such as gender-sexuality alliances and Black student alliances.

Branching these norms out to other teams at the site would be a natural next step.

As you plan and dream about this work, I want to offer a consideration. We have looked at the difference between inviting people to the table and engaging and communicating authentically with all stakeholders through open systems that offer access and transparency. However, equity shifts can be brilliant in process and fail in implementation because of what happens after the discussion. Here's an example. Let's say you hold ongoing forums to solicit feedback from parents and community members about a choice between curriculum A and curriculum B. You are intentional and specific, and there is clear evidence from the members that steers the committee toward curriculum choice A. But the district goes with curriculum B because that's what the "decider," department head, or some such single appointed person chooses. These are the moments where the rubber meets the road. We have all been in situations where someone asked for our voice but it was not respected or listened to in any way. If we are going to truly make an equity shift in the system, the process of gathering feedback is extremely important, but the ultimate decision and implementation must be a part of the equity shift, too. Use figure 3.3 to track your own plan for how team processes and actions can shift to include equity.

Planning Guide for Teams and Formally Arranged Spaces		
How can team processes or actions shift to include equity?		
Team	Processes or Actions	Equity Shift

Figure 3.3: Equity shifts for teams and formally arranged spaces.

Visit **go.SolutionTree.com/diversityandequity** for a free reproducible version of this figure.

Tool

Courageous Conversations About Race by Glenn E. Singleton (2015)
offers norms, agreements, and conditions for how to have
difficult conversations centering race.
Visit https://courageousconversation.com/about to access this tool.

CONCLUSION

In this chapter, we focused on ways to structure equity within our existing teams and systems, beginning with broadening our definition of stakeholders—recognizing, for example, that we can effect change by working not only with students, classroom teachers, and families but with those in positions that often get overlooked, such as receptionists and data managers. We also hearkened back to the idea of getting proximate, destabilizing the incredibly harmful party host–party guest dynamic that can sometimes mark equity work by encouraging the dominant, self-appointed decision makers to go where the marginalized groups are rather than "inviting them to the table." Finally, we took a closer look at making equity shifts within teams with the goal of changing our systems to be more open and accessible.

KEY TAKEAWAYS

Here's what to do to make the most of what we've covered in each section of this chapter.

Incorporate Multiple Stakeholders

- Be comprehensive and intentional when identifying stakeholders.
- Elevate voices of marginalized groups.
- Eliminate the party host–party guest dynamic, and create new ways to engage with your stakeholders.

Shift Team Goals and Processes

- Identify what teams you already have.
- Specify and practice an equity shift in at least one team's processes and actions.
- Identify (potential) open systems in your school and district.

4

EVIDENT EQUITY
Live It Out

The academy is not paradise. But learning is a
place where paradise can be created. The classroom, with all
its limitations, remains a location of possibility.

—bell hooks

Evident equity is the tangible, living, breathing examples of equity living out in your school or district. Evident equity is the feeling of the school culture, the artwork on the walls, and the processes for team meetings. When you have the mission statement but not the action, the work becomes less impactful and more convoluted. Clear evidence of equity is another avenue for how this work becomes ingrained in the culture and climate of our schools and districts. One of my favorite professors told me, "You should be able to walk into a school or a classroom and know who the students are that go there—when the kids are not even there" (S. Wolf, personal communication, 2004). The implications of this statement are that the identities and cultures of students and who they are should be all around us. This is about the heroes we celebrate on posters and what voices we include in books and materials. It's students bringing in family pictures to hang on the walls of the classroom because they see themselves as a part of it.

This fourth and final quadrant in the equity heat map is just what it sounds like: the ways in which equity is evident in your environment—walls, signage, messaging, curriculum choices, and more. Evident equity overlaps with all three of the other quadrants in that they all really boil down to what our efforts have produced. That is why this book's title is drawn from that fourth quadrant. Can students, teachers, and other stakeholders *see* and *feel* equity when they interact with the school? Have all systems within the school, from the top down, truly embraced equity? Has equity been embedded in foundations of everything the school does?

To make sure these goals become reality, we must ensure our schools have laid the proper groundwork. From there, we can consider ways to embed equity to make sure it is evident in every facet of the school environment.

GROUNDWORK

When teachers plan a lesson, they have state, local, or federal standards they are grounded in. These standards are the scaffolding and backbone for their lessons and units. The standards provide not only a road map but also a foundation for future learning. Standards, in addition to pacing guides and scheduled testing, largely guide what educators will do in their classrooms. Similarly, with equity work, we need a solid groundwork on which to build. This groundwork is composed of the district's or school's core beliefs, values, mission statements, and more, and all of these elements provide the weight and authority for us to continue this work.

I can't tell you how many times I have referred teachers and worried principals to their school district's core beliefs when they raise concerns about an equity issue. I ask them whether the lesson or conversation can firmly be aligned with one of those beliefs. If they say yes, then we know the support is there: they are aligning their work with the district's beliefs. This alignment provides some sense of security, as well as a guiding light. For instance, a teacher who was covering a unit that included a text about Jackie Robinson was concerned about the language used in that text (that is, *African American*, *Black*, *Negro*, and the N-word). The teacher decided the class was going to skip over these parts and not address them for fear of parent or student pushback. We worked instead to align the conversation with district beliefs, content standards, and best practices around speaking and listening and courageous dialogue. In doing so, the teacher was able to contact parents about upcoming language and give them resources for approaching the text and having conversations with their children. Additionally, the class was able to hold a rich discussion about words, their purpose, and how they change—or stay stagnant—over time. Your school or district may have core beliefs, or it may have a strategic plan. Whatever form it takes, the importance of having solid backing when conducting equity work cannot be overstated.

Tool

Look to your school or district mission statement or public-facing plan. Does it include equity or antiracist goals? If not, does your state have social-emotional or health and wellness standards that address inclusion and access? Use this exercise as a tool to either make goals for how your school, district, or state policies could be amended or to lay your groundwork for evident equity in your school using existing policies.

One important part of laying the groundwork to live out equity is to consider whether your district has created an overarching equity policy or goal and whether the district personnel have been systemically trained for that goal. When equity is living out, it has actions and some weight behind it: putting your time and money where your mouth is, per se. Your equity policy has to be apparent, but even more so, it has to have teeth. Does it disrupt any current practices? Who will be trained on what that policy means (and does not mean)? Does the same policy that espouses antiracism also disrupt racist hiring practices? Does your inclusion statement also ensure interpreters at your board meetings? It is the *follow-up* to the equity statement that ensures it will be taken seriously. Every year, educators sit through any number of mandatory updates and trainings to stay within compliance and policy. These trainings receive precious bandwidth. But what about equity policy? What about antiracist non-negotiables and expectations for diversity and inclusion? To fully communicate the gravity of what we talk about, we must also accompany it with action.

EMBEDDED EQUITY

One of the best teachers I ever worked with, Ricki Jo Scott, created a classroom that was inclusive and culturally responsive in such authentic and meaningful ways. She was an elementary special education teacher, and her classroom was so joyful and accessible. She took pictures of her students working through routines and different activities and then posted those pictures where the students would need them, as step-by-step reminders. She used smiling pictures of other staff and students at the school to explain words and letters in their names. For one unit on community, she drove through the neighborhood filming different landmarks her students would recognize: the barbershop, the library, the sundial. The class then created a huge map together that taught the students about social studies standards like cardinal directions, community resources, and helpers. By including their neighborhoods and cultures in the lesson, Ricki Jo highlighted her students' identities in an interdisciplinary and affirming way, truly showing evident equity.

We don't need the students themselves in front of us to know who the school community is. Ricki Jo's classroom itself is a tangible representation of her belief in culturally sustaining pedagogy. Our values can drive everything outward facing about our schools and offices, from the signage to the curriculum to the environment. What would it feel like to walk into a school and know that it is an antiracist space? What would a school district office feel like when equity is living out loud? In the introduction, I shared with you the quote from Arundhati Roy (2020), who urges us to "imagine another world." Here is your chance: embedded equity is where equity and antiracist ideals come to fruition in the world around us.

Table 4.1 (page 62) includes a list that my colleagues and I have compiled. While not comprehensive, it does give a broad picture of just how many places equity can

Table 4.1: Embedded-Equity Reflection Questions

Embedded Equity Living It Out			
Is equity evident?			
School Spaces	Reflection Questions	District Spaces	Reflection Questions
Field trips	Who has access to this trip? What barriers are there? Is the trip to a place that is culturally and emotionally safe for all students?	Social media	What voices are being amplified on what platform? What culture is centered?
Discipline	What avenues are available for students to relearn and practice behavior expectations?	Communication	What is the process for determining what is important to send communication about?
Curriculum	Are materials reflective of the student population? Do all students have access to materials at both school and home?	Curriculum	Do materials explicitly align with districtwide antiracist goals and strategic plans?
School spaces	Are spaces representative of student and family demographics? Are students involved in the creation of the space? Do materials within spaces explicitly state that all communities are welcome and safe?	Signage	Is signage available in the languages other than English spoken in the district? Are the images used in signage actual district students and staff? What are best practices for safe spaces for LGBTQ+ students and families? (See appendix B, page 81, for more ways to support the LGBTQ+ community.)
Celebrations	What intentional planning and research has taken place to ensure that all students have equal opportunity to win awards? Are award winners representative of your population? Are there checks in place so that student success is not reliant on teacher recommendation alone?	Staff recognition	How are staff awarded, and what for? Are there any specific antiracist or equity recognitions? What staff have been historically given awards, and do they make up an accurate sampling of the district community?

live out within a system. Table 4.1 also offers some guiding reflection questions for your planning; the questions are designed to prompt thinking about how the space is or isn't living out your equity goals.

The following examples demonstrate how evident equity can live out in elementary curriculum, middle school disciplinary practices, and high school walls.

Elementary Example

Not long after I started as the director of equity affairs for Wake County Public Schools in 2018, I wrote on Twitter about the cultural appropriation of Indigenous people during Thanksgiving celebrations. I was tired of seeing elementary students dressed up as "Indians" and Pilgrims against the backdrop of a happy-go-lucky narrative of the first Thanksgiving. I urged teachers to tell their students the truth about our country's relationship with Indigenous people and to not use cute activities to reduce an entire race of people to a false stereotype. As it turned out, the tweet, shown in figure 4.1, went viral, garnering thousands of likes and retweets that triggered news stories and other social media platforms to share the message. Now, this tweet felt commonsensical to me, but I quickly realized that cultural appropriation was something we simply were not addressing in our classrooms and in expectations as a culture. Some replies attacked me by imagining that I hate Thanksgiving and am trying to indoctrinate youth.

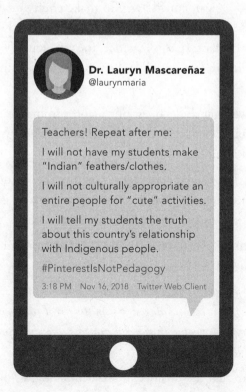

Dr. Lauryn Mascareñaz
@laurynmaria

Teachers! Repeat after me:

I will not have my students make "Indian" feathers/clothes.

I will not culturally appropriate an entire people for "cute" activities.

I will tell my students the truth about this country's relationship with Indigenous people.

#PinterestIsNotPedagogy

3:18 PM   Nov 16, 2018   Twitter Web Client

Source: Mascareñaz, 2018.

Figure 4.1: Tweet.

I write all this background to say that, yes, speaking up about old practices can be risky. As an equity leader, you may find yourself in the middle of a debate about what educators are used to doing and what you are asking them to do. Saying, "We have always done it this way" is dangerous language in education. Maya Angelou (as cited in Winfrey, n.d.) tells us, "When you know better, you do better." We *know* better than to make costumes out of people's culture. We *know* that it is not grounded in pedagogy or learning standards, so we have to *do* better. In the years since I posted that tweet, especially every November when it resurfaces, I receive so many emails and handwritten letters from educators and parents across the country who have told me this offered a new perspective for them they had not considered. One teacher told me that she still thought Pilgrim hats were cute but that, after reading more about the context, she had decided she would make turkey hats instead. Another educator wrote asking for a reliable source for finding authentic American Indian children's books (the answer is American Indians in Children's Literature [https://bit.ly/3lYYM9N], a great resource from Debbie Reese of the Nambé Pueblo). A student who is a member of the Lumbee Tribe of North Carolina sent me a message on Twitter, telling me about how she is proud to be a jingle-dress dancer and wished more teachers would see her as she is.

To actually see change happen and hear students say how much it means to them is a potent experience. This is the power of voice. This is the power of speaking up and saying what matters—a clear, concise way to make equity evident in many spaces. Whether it's on Twitter, in a staff meeting, or with family at the dinner table, this is how change becomes evident. In this instance, the way equity was evident and living out during Thanksgiving in many schools changed simply because people were engaging in new conversations.

Review figure 4.2, which includes questions adapted from those that diversity, equity, and inclusion consultant Kim Tran (2016) has crafted, to help you plan your celebrations, spirit weeks, and holidays while avoiding unintentional cultural appropriation.

If we take a look at the arts and crafts activities from the Thanksgiving example, we can move through these questions to determine if an activity is culturally appropriated. Let's think about construction paper feather headdresses, for example.

- To what ethnic, racial, or cultural group does the practice or artifact belong?

  The first Thanksgiving narrative centers on the Mashpee and Aquinnah Wampanoag, but this headdress is a mash-up of commonly held stereotypes about Indigenous people in general and may not be representative of their traditional dress.

- Is the group that the practice or artifact belongs to oppressed? If so, how?

  Yes, Indigenous people were massacred and systemically removed from their land, which they continue to fight for to this day.

Five Questions to Avoid Cultural Appropriation	
Question	**Your Response**
To what ethnic, racial, or cultural group does the practice or artifact belong?	
Is the group that the practice or artifact belongs to oppressed? If so, how?	
Do you benefit from using this practice or artifact? If so, how?	
Why might the practice or artifact make someone uncomfortable?	
What makes it possible for you to engage with this practice, tradition, or material? For instance, is your economic or social privilege your introduction to it?	

Source: Adapted from Tran, 2016.

Figure 4.2: Reflection questions to avoid cultural appropriation.

- Do you benefit from using this practice or artifact? If so, how?

  Yes, I benefit because it is an easy craft for my students to make, and I have always used it—so it is accessible, and I don't need to prep for a new lesson.

- Why might the practice or artifact make someone uncomfortable?

  If there is an Indigenous person in my class or in my school family, they could be uncomfortable with this craft because it is incorrect or insensitive.

- What makes it possible for you to engage with this practice, tradition, or material? For instance, is your economic or social privilege your introduction to it?

  I have the readily purchased and created store-bought materials for this craft instead of foraging and using natural and organic materials as the culture intended.

Middle School Example

My friend Ryan Williams is a leader in many aspects: as an educator, learner, consultant, and assistant principal. He is a strong voice for equity and can be found at any and every training or gathering that is education or equity related. One of Ryan's keenest skills is creating space for healing and relationship building within his school. As a huge proponent of *restorative justice* (the practice of repairing relationships, acknowledging harm, and decreasing disciplinary actions), Ryan worked over the years to build out a program at his previous middle school that has reduced suspensions by more than half. Even though Ryan's school was largely Black and Brown students, there was still a disproportionality in referrals and suspensions between BIPOC and White students.

Ryan built a great deal of capacity and skill at his school; in fact, many of the staff are now able to guide students, staff, and families through the restorative-circle practice instead of relying on administration solely. A restorative circle, according to the International Institute for Restorative Practices (n.d.), is:

> A versatile restorative practice that can be used proactively, to develop relationships and build community or reactively, to respond to wrongdoing, conflicts and problems. Circles give people an opportunity to speak and listen to one another in an atmosphere of safety, decorum and equality.

A restorative circle is a group, large or small, in which the participants sit in a physical circle and go through guided questions and acknowledgments with a facilitator. Ryan worked with a group of students from the time they started at his school in sixth grade to support them in their own leadership skills, with the goal of having them become the facilitators of the circle in eighth grade. This way, the circles become truly student-led and -directed. This restorative-practice implementation is such a part of the school now that other educators from surrounding schools are asking to watch Ryan in order to learn about restorative-circle best practices and his path to leading for restorative justice.

In chapter 2 (page 25), we covered how we build out our equity coalition by slowly increasing the capacity of those who are doing the work. Ryan was acting on the school's mission to be more equitable in its discipline practices and to amplify the voices of its BIPOC students through circles, but he is *also* serving as a model to others who wish to do equity work in their own areas. He has built out an equity space for restorative justice that is powerful and will remain synonymous with that middle school.

This model of learning from those who are actively doing the day-to-day work is another intentional point of evident equity. The learning and growth can be dictated from a school or district leader in a top-down fashion, but learning can also instead (and arguably more powerfully so) be interwoven in a latticelike fashion, with roots deeply embedded in the equity work educators are already bravely leading.

High School Example

One of the high schools in my district debuted a powerful mural in the fall of 2020. Principal Karen Summers worked with her art teacher, Slater Mapp, and local artist Sean Kernick to co-create a piece to memorialize the inaugural year of the school. The school's predominate demographic is a wealthy and White Christian population, with small groups of Muslim, Black, and Latino/a students. In addition to considering the yearly student survey the district administered, Karen was intentional about having informal and formal conversations with students at her school. Karen knew from these conversations that BIPOC students at her school were not feeling seen or heard. So, from the earliest iteration of the project, Karen felt strongly that the mural should showcase her students of color.

Sean worked with small groups of students to teach them about wall art as one of the earliest forms of recorded history from ancient civilizations, and he prompted them to discuss their mural plans by asking, "If people looked back on this year one thousand years from now, what would they see?" At first, the mural was in a different form altogether. Then, when racial unrest and pandemic anxiety overtook the United States, the principal took a hard stance that the content depicted in the mural had to shift. Even though they were already midway through planning, the team members agreed that they had to include authentic representations of the U.S. climate at the time.

What happened after that was a true act of collaboration and community as students identified topics and turned them into symbols. Sean educated high school students on the roots of spray paint and wall art as forms of protest and activism. Eventually, the images students were deciding on and creating started coming to life on the walls. Students were included in the creative process of mapping, sketching, and painting the mural, down to the smallest details of how a ponytail would swing for a volleyball player. Staff contributed too, with the band instructor pointing out that no one played the violin at the school yet, so they should pick another instrument instead. What resulted is a diverse and representative piece of artwork, which graces the main hallway of the new high school. For a panoramic view of this colorful, vibrant mural, see https://bit.ly/3863xGz for the school's Twitter post featuring it.

As photos documenting the mural's progress went up on social media, the project received high praise. However, as is almost always the case with equity work, there was resistance as well. Slater and the rest of the team were bombarded with phone calls, emails, and concerns from a small but vocal part of the school community. The pushback revolved mostly around proposed images of students wearing masks, a Muslim student in the center, the inclusion of a Black Lives Matter shirt, and the like. But the artist and team doubled down on their belief in their students' vision and how it was being received by students every day. Sean stated, "I love the idea of making a student feel more comfortable. Students are saying that this literally changed the way they felt about coming to school" (S. Kernick, personal communication, December 18, 2020).

CONCLUSION

In this chapter, we discussed the groundwork on which our equity work must be built: our school's or district's mission, vision, and values, which we can refer back to as we make the needed changes throughout our organization. We also got to the heart of evident equity, starting to piecing together everything we've learned to help guarantee our district or school space is filled with visible signs of the work we've undertaken, as well as true, life-affirming representations of all our staff and students.

KEY TAKEAWAYS

Here's what to do to make the most of what we've covered in each section of this chapter.

Groundwork

- Determine what guiding beliefs or statements will serve as the foundation for your work.

Embedded Equity

- Think about how equity is living and breathing all around you; it is more than words.

- Imagine what your school or district could look like in a truly equitable world.

- Make small but impactful changes to everyday parts of your system.

- Speak up against the way things have always been done.

5

STAND FIRM
Equity Leadership in
the Face of Resistance

You become strong by doing the things
you need to be strong for.

—*Audre Lorde*

We have looked at how difficult engaging in equity and antiracist work is. Whether you are leading the work on your own or are part of a team, it is exhausting and trying work. But what about when your coalition is small and the resistance is large? How does equity leadership play out when faced with naysayers, doubters, and outright defiance to antiracist goals? Overcoming such resistance is at its heart a difficult endeavor. In this chapter, we will address how to have a sense of the larger sociocultural and sociopolitical factors that impact equity work, as well as discuss the grounding concept of supporting students that will help to keep you centered as you confront roadblocks to your progress.

SOCIOPOLITICAL CONTEXT OF EQUITY WORK

In chapter 2 (page 25), we discussed how to keep people in the zone of disequilibrium. This is the sweet spot where people are just uncomfortable enough to learn and grow but not so uncomfortable that they will avoid the work and tap out. I used the analogy of cooking—turning up the heat and turning down the heat. As equity leaders, we create opportunities for disequilibrium (turning up the heat) while staying ready with structure and taking on responsibility ourselves in order to decrease the heat. To stretch that analogy a little further, each system has a boiling point. The *boiling point* is when the work becomes too much for the system to absorb and process, and the work either stops or erupts into conflict. When leaders push equity work to the boiling point, there will be backlash. There will be stakeholders who push back and hinder progress, and it will feel as though the work is stalled. Further, resistance can take many forms: a skewed media story, community opposition, bureaucratic holdups, or blatant resistance, such as graffiti, slurs, or hate crimes.

This boiling point is different with each system. Some school districts can withstand the heat of multiple changes at once and have a culture that supports rapid growth. Other districts may have a culture that is ready for just one incremental change at a time. Schools are very much the same; knowing your staff and their comfort level with topics will be essential to determining how far you can push their learning before they move out of the zone of disequilibrium. Some potential boiling points could be empty rhetoric or community outrage over so-called "critical race theory" being taught in K–12 schools, or it could be the culmination of sustained equity and antiracist work that has led to work-avoidance. If the rhetoric is empty and holds no standing in your school or district—as is the case with debates over critical race theory—then hold firm to the course you are on and keep pushing. This backlash is not in direct opposition to your work but instead a large-scale and coordinated attempt to misname and misrepresent how history is taught in schools. If the boiling point is a genuine reaction to the strategic antiracist work you are doing, then you can consider a coordinated response. Review the reflection questions in figure 5.1 as you consider your own system. These will help guide you in determining when or whether you may reach a boiling point.

Knowing the sociocultural and political context of where you work and educate is essential. I cannot emphasize this enough. Schools and districts are not operating in a vacuum. We are a part of a much larger societal context. When I was teaching in the Bay Area of California, the educators in our Bayview–Hunter's Point neighborhood of San Francisco embedded culturally responsive pedagogy and equity into our work in a way that I have not encountered in my career since. At San Francisco Unified, my principal, Tamitrice Rice-Mitchell, was a strong leader for culturally responsive teaching. She made sure that we all received training in culturally responsive pedagogy. Any time new staff joined the team, they took the same training from educator Sharroky Hollie to ensure we all had the same foundational understanding.

One year, Ms. Rice-Mitchell modeled a new engagement protocol at each staff meeting. As teachers, we were then given the materials—such as extra chart paper or an offer to print our photos—and the charge of trying out this new strategy over the course of the month. By the end of the year, I had nine different culturally responsive engagement strategies in my toolbox, including how to use music in my formative assessments and a wide array of call-and-response options. My instructional toolbox grew exponentially and my students were engaged like never before. I started to see

Reflection Question	Response
If you had to guess, what do you think is your system's boiling point?	
What is staff's comfort level with conversations around sensitive topics like race and gender?	
What does educator stakeholder support look like regarding equity work?	
Do you have family, caregiver, and local community support? What does that support or the lack of it look like?	
What is your relationship with local media?	
Is there district or administrative support for equity initiatives? What does that support or the lack of it look like?	
What topics are considered taboo and not talked about?	
Is there a process for speaking up about prejudice and injustice? If so, what is it?	

Figure 5.1: Boiling-point reflection questions.

*Visit **go.SolutionTree.com/diversityandequity** for a free reproducible version of this figure.*

how these culturally responsive strategies were changing outcomes for my students, providing a higher level of academic achievement for them. In the Bayview, equity meant that our team of educators had to teach in such a way that our students would authentically connect to the curriculum *and* to us, and culturally responsive strategies did that. This level of readiness among many team members was due not only to the incredible staff and the leadership of Ms. Rice-Mitchell but also to the sociocultural context of the Bay Area, which was largely liberal and diverse and often a leader in race, LGBTQ+, and immigration policy (although not without its own hiccups and issues, I assure you). Spending our professional development funds on culturally responsive teaching or dedicating entire staff meetings to how to connect with our entirely BIPOC community was encouraged in this climate, both by district administration and the families of our students. In many other sociocultural contexts, these initiatives would require vast undertakings to launch.

Now, working in education since 2016 in the U.S. South means I am keenly aware of how different the sociocultural landscape is from San Francisco. Policy and media look very different here. Oftentimes, the community is ready for conversations about race but not about LGBTQ+ support. Or when election season heightens conversations around race and immigration, we see a surge in school and community conflict.

I know that in order to make progress for our LGBTQ+ community, I have to be much more strategic and intentional in my work and be able to adapt to shifts in our national political context around policy changes with Title IX (which protects people from sex-based discrimination in education programs or activities that receive federal financial assistance) and Title VI (which prohibits discrimination on the basis of race, color, or national origin in any program or activity that receives federal financial assistance; Every Student Succeeds Act, 2015). When Supreme Court circuit decisions arise, I must move quickly to make sure we incorporate changes into our own policy and training. For example, in 2020, the U.S. Court of Appeals for the Fourth Circuit decided in favor of transgender student Gavin Grimm in *Grimm v. Gloucester County School Board*. The decision means that states under the Fourth Circuit jurisdiction must comply with affirming transgender students, providing access to bathrooms that align with a student's gender identity, and ensuring coverage under the equal protection clause of the U.S. Constitution (*Grimm v. Gloucester County School Board*, 2020). Since the Fourth Circuit covers the state in which I work, I worked alongside our legal counsel and senior leadership team to ensure that we updated our harassment policy in a timely manner, and then I sat in on our board of education vote to include the words *gender identity* in our harassment and bullying policy in case questions arose. The next step after voting on our new board policy language was creating learning for our staff about what exactly those protections and wording mean in an educational setting. Having a finger on the pulse of legal decisions like this helps you better maneuver and implement change.

So how do we stay strong in the face of resistance? How do we hold true to what we believe in and continue to fight for it? How do we constructively confront the naysayers? I would offer three potential pathways that you can use in isolation or in tandem with others in order to stay the course for your harbor.

1. **Highlight** connections between equity work and district beliefs and policy.

2. **Connect** with your coalition to be thought partners and public-facing advocates.

3. **Center** students in actions and decisions.

By doing varied combinations of these, we stand firm in our equity decisions and leverage the support and scaffolds that are in place. For example, in the context of supporting our LGBTQ+ students, our team was able to do all three: we (1) highlighted the connection with our district bullying and harassment policy, (2) activated our coalition to connect with team members and others about how nuances of this policy, such as pronouns and deadnaming, would live out in practice, and (3) centered the voices of students who were marginalized as we looked for immediate solutions that would support them. Table 5.1 gives you an idea of how standing firm could look in different scenarios.

Table 5.1: Actions to Take in the Face of Backlash

Standing Firm Equity Leadership in the Face of Resistance	
Backlash	**Potential Actions**
A negative media story on the school's equity work	• Highlight connection between the issue and district goals and beliefs through official district communication and with media or press release. • Connect with leadership teams to reinforce the message within their respective departments or committees.
Negative community opinions, letters, and calls	• Call on your coalition to speak up in their respective spaces or media they feel comfortable utilizing (connect). The voices of naysayers are often the loudest, but they are not the only voices.
Racist or prejudicial incident	• Ensure the safety and support of the targeted student or group (center). • Designate established teams to respond to the incident from their team perspectives (connect). • Gather a coalition to firmly denounce the act in official district communication (connect).
Lack of green light from administration or board on an equity initiative, such as professional development courses	• Create a case for supporting the initiative, highlighting alignment to goals and vision as well as content standards. • Identify and make a case for how this initiative will directly support and affect students (center).

Tool

Responding to Hate and Bias at School (Learning for Justice, 2017) is a guide for administrators to use in response to a bias or racist incident. It is broken down into three sections: (1) before a crisis occurs, (2) when there's a crisis, and (3) after the worst is over. Visit www.learningforjustice.org/magazine/publications /responding-to-hate-and-bias-at-school to access this tool.

WHEN IN DOUBT, CENTER THE STUDENTS

We often forget the stakeholders at the center of all these decisions: students. My dear colleague and friend Teresa Bunner often reminds our team that without students, none of us would have jobs. We joke about spending too much time with adults and not enough time with students. Teresa is a master at reminding us that students are at the center of all we do. Being an equity leader means being proximate to those students and families who are experiencing the inequity and remembering that we cannot make decisions *for* people without a deep understanding of who they are and their own lived experience.

Being an equity leader also means that when in doubt, we center our support for students in our actions. When confusion and major decisions happen, we must *center the students and keep them at the forefront of the conversation*. In our transgender example, for instance, this means centering the experience and often harsh reality of being a transgender student in a school. This means that while there will be opinions and policy and much debate, we direct our focus to what will remove barriers and create a supportive, welcoming environment for this student. An example of this is when remote learning was the norm during the beginning of the 2020 COVID-19 pandemic and many transgender students were having to attend online classes with their dead names—that is, their given names that do not align with their gender identity (for instance, Emily could be Emerson's dead name), and displayed on the screen for all to see. This was awful and terribly traumatic for many students. Resolving this issue can entail a huge technology and school data system conversation around preferred names and pronouns that could be ongoing for quite some time. But in the interim, what supports our students *now*? They cannot and should not wait for the bureaucratic wheels of the system to turn. Can they use different email addresses? Can the teacher encourage all students in the class to pick what names they want to display? These types of student-centered questions will help to realign yourself with the core of your equity work.

Equity is a hot topic or a buzzword. The swell of emails and phone calls I get about support for any number of equity-adjacent topics directly coincides with the state of our country and what news stories the media are covering. Yes, many of us are spurred to action as we see injustice unfold before our eyes. But it is not enough to simply engage in equity work for the sake of it or because it is a buzzword. I urge you to find your own why for doing this work. In the face of resistance, knowing your why will be the most grounding concept you have in your toolbox. Write it down. Put it on a sticky note where you can see it. Hang the picture of that student or your own child who inspires your why for doing this work. In case it is helpful to work through your why, I have provided some guiding questions to assist you in figure 5.2. Many of us get into this work because we are called to enact change. At the very beginning of the book, we looked at how equity work is not the next best thing—it is *the* thing. It is truly a state of mind, a set of values, how we talk to people, and how we see students and families. As we work to shift structures, mindsets, teams, and environments, our why will guide us. We will find that equity is *the* thing that is guiding these shifts, these decisions, and this work.

My Why	
Why do I want to embark on equity and antiracist work?	
Take some time to quietly reflect on the preceding prompt. What follows are some guiding questions to help your thinking.	
What are my values about education?	
What do I believe about students and their potential?	
What is the role of community in education?	
What is the role of families in education?	
What is privilege? What is educational privilege?	
What inequities are there in my school or district?	
Am I antiracist?	
What is the difference between equity and equality?	

Figure 5.2: My why.

*Visit **go.SolutionTree.com/diversityandequity** for a free reproducible version of this figure.*

CONCLUSION

In this book, I have given you strong examples of what systemwide equity can look like. Throughout the previous chapters, we have discussed organizational, shared, structured, and evident equity. We have worked through dozens of reflection questions to determine our stakeholders, our processes and shifts, and our why. We began our exploration of equity with the equity heat map (see figure I.1, page 5) and the guiding premise that equity cannot live in a single space. Equity *must* permeate the entire school, the entire district. When we relegate equity work to a single task or staff member, it can never become more than just a team.

So, while we seek to change the systems, we must also work to change ourselves. Take the time to explore your identity and how it shows up in your values and beliefs about education. Remember why you started in education and why you continue to do it. Embarking on and leading an equity journey has no destination—there is no stopping point. There will always be more to fight for when it comes to what is best for all our students. But, as educators, we know what it is to see and make meaningful change every day in service to the future. So equity work, in many ways, is second nature to us. That means a deep commitment to what our students and our communities deserve and the lengths we are willing to go to in order to ensure a better outcome for them. Doing intentional and authentic equity and antiracist work is about creating a different world that dismantles systems of oppression *and* fundamentally changes who we are. So, equity leader: Keep rising. Keep imagining that new world. I am proud to be in the fight with you.

KEY TAKEAWAYS

Here's what to do to make the most of what we've covered in each section of this chapter.

Sociopolitical Context of Equity Work

- Reflect on the sociopolitical context in which you are working and possible boiling points.
- Highlight, connect, and center.

When in Doubt, Center the Students

- Center students in decisions, conversations, and actions.
- Spend some time with your why.

APPENDIX A
Sample Policies and Resolutions

The following pieces of policy and board resolutions are examples of educational institutions creating formal structures to promote equity. They serve as model language for schools and districts that may be looking to enact similar policy or supports. I will highlight three examples through throughout the United States: (1) Oregon, (2) Maryland, and (3) Ohio.

OREGON DEPARTMENT OF EDUCATION: BLACK LIVES MATTER

In the wake of the George Floyd killing and racial equality protests all over the world, many schools and districts prepared formal statements condemning racism. The resolution in figure A.1, however, by the Oregon Department of Education (2020), goes farther to explicitly support Black Lives Matter. It was also accompanied by a letter signed by the education organizations in the state. It starts with a bold and simple statement and then leads directly into the charge from students that educators must work to repair the damage done by racial injustice. This resolution is an example of bold action; indeed, many institutions denounced racism but would not endorse the often-divisive Black Lives Matter movement. The emphasis in the opening line of being accountable to students is an example of what centering students can look like, as I discussed in chapter 5 (page 69). Go to https://bit.ly/3idZ4I1 to access the full resolution.

BLACK LIVES MATTER RESOLUTION

October 15, 2020

WHEREAS, Black Lives Matter; and

WHEREAS, the Oregon State Board of Education is charged by students to continue the real work of repairing the damage of racial injustice, brutality, and hatred by bringing messages of understanding, love, and belonging more fully to our schools throughout Oregon; and

WHEREAS, the State Board of Education's mission is to provide leadership and vision for Oregon's schools and districts by enacting equitable policies and promoting educational practices that lead directly to the educational and life success of all Oregon PK–12 students; and

WHEREAS, the State Board of Education promotes nondiscrimination and an environment free of harassment based on an individual's race, color, religion, sex, sexual orientation, gender identity or expression, national original, marital status, age, or disability

---

Source: Oregon Department of Education, 2020.

Figure A.1: Excerpt from Oregon Department of Education resolution.

FREDERICK COUNTY PUBLIC SCHOOLS, MARYLAND: TRANSGENDER AND GENDER-NONCONFORMING STUDENTS

The policy in figure A.2 uses the language and terminology it advocates that educators use, as reflected by its title (using the term gender-nonconforming) and the wording within the policy (a pertinent example). It begins with a statement of protected status and accomplishes a strategic connection to other policies already in place—in this case, bullying and harassment. You can find the full text at https://bit .ly/3ceraiO, along with a video explaining the policy.

POLICY | BOARD OF EDUCATION OF FREDERICK COUNTY, MARYLAND

| CREATING WELCOMING AND AFFIRMING SCHOOLS FOR TRANSGENDER AND GENDER-NONCONFORMING STUDENTS | POLICY 443 |

443.1 Purpose

Gender identity is a protected status in Frederick County Public Schools (FCPS). The purpose of this policy is to prevent discrimination, stigmatization, harassment, and bullying of students who are transgender or who are gender nonconforming and to create school cultures that are safe, welcoming, and affirming for all students. This policy is also designed to ensure that all students have the opportunity to express themselves and live authentically.

Bullying, harassment, and intimidation based on perceived or real sex, sexual orientation, or gender identity or expression is prohibited by FCPS (see Board Policy 437). FCPS addresses bullying, harassment, and intimidation in compliance with its disciplinary policies and regulations, which includes education and providing students and staff with appropriate resources and supports. The Board of Education (Board) acknowledges that the transfer of students who are victims of bullying, harassment, or intimidation to a different school is not a preferred mode of responding and such response should only be considered in consultation, agreement, or at the request of the victim and his/her parent or legal guardian.

Source: Board of Education of Frederick County, Maryland, 2019.

Figure A.2: Excerpt from Frederick County Public Schools transgender and gender-nonconforming student policy.

CINCINNATI PUBLIC SCHOOLS: EQUITY

The policy in figure A.3 provides context at the beginning for *why* such a policy is necessary, including language on predictability, perpetuation of disparities, and equitable access. The policy also includes a board resolution of working definitions for *diversity*, *equity*, *inclusion*, and *excellence in education*. Visit https://bit.ly/3ie9M1f to access the full text.

Board Policy 2255 | Equity and Excellence in Education

Our students, staff and stakeholders bring their personal backgrounds into our schools and the District is richer for it. Each of them has a legitimate expectation to have a barrier-free learning environment counteracting the contemporary and historical impact of bias, prejudice, and discrimination which for generations has produced a predictability of learning outcomes based on race, class, socioeconomics, gender, ethnicity, sexual orientation, gender identity, cognitive/physical ability, diverse language fluency, and religion.

It is the obligation of the District to embrace the diversity within our District while actively eliminating practices that perpetuate the disparities among our students so that all students have the opportunity to benefit equally. These disparities are unacceptable and are directly at odds with the Board's Vision that Cincinnati Public Schools "is a community that ensures equitable access to a world class education unleashing the potential of every student."

In order to secure this vision, the District will focus on the individual and unique needs of each student. Therefore, the Board established the following course of action:

- Foster the universal values as expressed and adopted in the attached *Board Resolution—Adopting Working Definitions for Diversity, Equity, Inclusion and Excellence in Education* so that these values are shared across the District by a wide range of students, staff, and stakeholders who are committed to act on these values without bias, prejudice, or discrimination.

- Commit to ensuring that fairness, equity, and inclusion are essential principles of our school system fully integrating these principles into all of our policies, programs, operations, and practices.

- Adopt a teaching and learning culture that includes high expectations of students and staff, varied teaching and learning styles, and individualized as well as systematic supports for teachers and students.

Source: Cincinnati Public Schools, 2017.

Figure A.3: Excerpt from Cincinnati Public Schools equity policy.

APPENDIX B
Suggested Further Reading and Resource Lists

The following resources are those I recommend the most when people ask me where to go for more support. These sites are all free to the public and are from leaders in each field. While this list is surely not the seminal or final word on how to support all of our students, many of these resources are created by educators and experts from marginalized communities themselves or from leading education organizations. I encourage you to vet your own resources and materials, consider sources, and find all the amazing ways people are working together to create change for our students.

CHILDREN AND YOUNG ADULT TEXT LISTS

A great way to incorporate equity into your classroom and school is through the intentional choices you make in texts and supporting curriculum. There are numerous book lists out there, but I find the following to be my go-to sites when I need a recommendation. My favorite thing about the majority of these resources is that they are examples of how to seek information and input from those closest to the inequity, such as Dr. Reese and her American Indians in Children's Literature site, and also of what representation or diverse literature looks like for them, such as the #DisruptTexts movement by and for teachers.

- **American Indians in Children's Literature (https://american indiansinchildrensliterature.blogspot.com):** Established in 2006 by Debbie Reese of the Nambé Pueblo, American Indians in Children's Literature (AICL) is a blog that is regularly updated with critical analysis of the presence of Indigenous peoples in children's and young adult books.

- **Embrace Race (www.embracerace.org/resources/childrens-books):** Embrace Race is dedicated to identifying, organizing, and, as needed, creating the tools, resources, discussion spaces, and networks needed to foster resilience in children of color; nurture inclusive, empathetic children of all races; raise kids who think critically about racial inequity; and support a movement of child and adult racial justice advocates for all children.

- **We Need Diverse Books (https://diversebooks.org/resources/where -to-find-diverse-books):** We Need Diverse Books is made up of a group of children's book lovers who are advocating for more diverse books and changes within the publishing industry. The site offers helpful tips about where to find books that are outside the status quo and includes rich, curated anthologies.

- **#DisruptTexts (https://disrupttexts.org):** Disrupt Texts is a grassroots effort led by a group of teachers who encourage other teachers to take a critical lens to the texts they use in the classroom. Their mission is to create a more representative and diverse language arts curriculum for students.

RESOURCE LIST FOR SERVING LGBTQ+ STUDENTS

Serving our LGBTQ+ students is often overlooked in school equity conversations. These resources will help guide you in creating more welcoming and inclusive schools for all students.

- **GLSEN (www.glsen.org/educator-resources):** GLSEN is a leader in how to best support and create LGBTQ+-inclusive schools. It offers guides to aid in instruction and curriculum choices, fostering a welcoming school or district climate, and supporting students.

- **Learning for Justice: Best Practices for Serving LGBTQ Students (www.learningforjustice.org/magazine/publications/best-practices -for-serving-lgbtq-students):** This guide highlights practices that educators can use in service of a safer and more validating school for LGBTQ+ students. It includes resources for open dialogue and representative curriculum.

- **Advocates for Youth: Creating Safer Spaces for LGBTQ Youth (www.advocatesforyouth.org/resources/curricula-education/creating -safer-spaces-for-lgbtq-youth):** Advocates for Youth works alongside thousands of young people in the United States and around the world as they fight for sexual health, rights, and justice.

- **PFLAG: Guide to Being a Straight Ally (https://pflag.org/publication /guidetobeingastraightally):** PFLAG works to combine education, advocacy, and support for the LGBTQ+ community members and their families and friends. This guide is full of great tips for straight allies who want to work to achieve equality for all.

- **Welcoming Schools: Responding to Children's Questions on LGBTQ Topics (www.welcomingschools.org/resources/challenging-questions):** Welcoming Schools, the education and youth branch of the Human Rights Campaign, created this guide for adults to practice responses to ensure that they are prepared to get students the answers they need.

SERVING IMMIGRANT AND REFUGEE STUDENTS

Immigrant and refugee students are often among the most vulnerable in our schools as they learn new languages, cultures, and customs while also recovering from their journeys to our classrooms. The following sites give valuable information for how to support the unique challenges of immigrant and refugee students.

- **National Association of School Psychologists: Supporting Refugee Children and Students—Tips for Educators (www.nasponline.org /resources-and-publications/resources-and-podcasts/school-climate -safety-and-crisis/mental-health-resources/war-and-terrorism /supporting-refugee-students):** This helpful site talks about the trauma many immigrant and refugee students have from resettlement and premigration events. It offers advice for how to include cultural norms when discussing mental health and advocates for a strengths-based approach.

- **¡Colorín Colorado! Immigration Guide (www.colorincolorado.org /immigration/guide):** This is a guide focused on helping immigrant students and their families feel safe and welcome in school communities. It includes many strategies, over fifty, and it is aimed at teachers, staff, and administrators.

- **American Federation of Teachers: Immigrant and Refugee Children (www.aft.org/sites/default/files/im_uac-educators-guide_2017.pdf):** This is a guide for those who teach undocumented or unaccompanied and refugee students. Educators can use it to help make sure that these students are receiving all the opportunities they need.

SERVING STUDENTS WHO ARE LEARNING ENGLISH

I am a firm believer that we should avoid labeling students with acronyms such as English learner (EL). They are students first, and they are learning English. Here are some notable organizations who cover the legal and instructional nuances of teaching students a second language.

- **National Education Association: English Language Learners: What You Need to Know (www.nea.org/professional-excellence /student-engagement/tools-tips/english-language-learners-what-you -need-know):** This National Education Association resource covers the legalities and implications of teaching students who are learning English. It also works to address the academic gap in data between native and non-native English-speaking students.

- **¡Colorín Colorado!: ELL Strategies and Best Practices (www.colorincolorado.org/ell-strategies-best-practices):** This is a tried-and-true organization that is a go-to for many educators when looking to support English language and literacy with students. It has lesson ideas, books lists, and approaches like how to use formative assessment techniques with students who are learning English.

FAMILY AND COMMUNITY ENGAGEMENT

Where do we go for help with our actions to authentically partner in our students' education? Here are some sites that will help spark ideas for engaging with families and communities.

- **U.S. Department of Education: Toolkit (https://ies.ed.gov/ncee /edlabs/projects/project.asp?projectID=4509):** Great resource from the Department of Education that has a wealth of activities and resources for educators to use in service to family and community engagement.

- **The Parent-Teacher Home Visit Project (www.pthvp.org):** The Parent-Teacher Home Visit Project is a grassroots model based on organizing principles of empowerment. PTHVP works to give educators resources for home visits that will build trust and communication with families.

- **The Dual Capacity-Building Framework for Family-School Partnerships (www.dualcapacity.org):** The Dual Capacity-Building Framework for Family-School Partnerships was developed by Karen L. Mapp and Eyal Bergman (2019). It is composed of research and identified best practices to support the development of family engagement. It acts like a compass to help guide educators toward the goals and outcomes they need to look for in order to make sure their family engagement efforts lead to student achievement.

REFERENCES

American Civil Liberties Union. (n.d.). *School-to-prison pipeline.* Accessed at www.aclu.org/issues /juvenile-justice/school-prison-pipeline/school-prison-pipeline-infographic on April 1, 2021.

Americans for Tax Fairness & Institute for Policy Studies. (2021, April 15). *Billionaire pandemic wealth gains of 55%, or $1.6 trillion, come amid three decades of rapid wealth growth.* Accessed at https://inequality.org/wp-content/uploads/2021/04/IPS-ATF-Billionaires-13-Month-31-Year -Report-copy.pdf on August 11, 2021.

Anderson, C. (2018). *We are not yet equal: Understanding our racial divide.* New York: Bloomsbury.

August, S. M. (2008). *Future protocol a.k.a. back to the future.* Accessed at www.school reforminitiative.org/download/future-protocol-a-k-a-back-to-the-future/ on August 13, 2021.

Benson, T. A., & Fiarman, S. E. (2020). *Unconscious bias in schools: A developmental approach to exploring race and racism* (Rev. ed.). Cambridge, MA: Harvard Education Press.

Black Lives Matter at School. (n.d.). *About.* Accessed at www.blacklivesmatteratschool.com/about .html on April 1, 2021.

Board of Education of Frederick County, Maryland. (2019, January 9). *Creating welcoming and affirming schools for transgender and gender nonconforming students.* Accessed at https://apps .fcps.org/legal/doc.php?number=443 on September 20, 2021.

Brockell, G. (2021, March 18). *The long, ugly history of anti-Asian racism and violence in the U.S.* Accessed at www.washingtonpost.com/history/2021/03/18/history-anti-asian-violence-racism on April 1, 2021.

Brosseau, L., & Dewing, M. (2009). *Canadian multiculturalism.* Accessed at https://lop.parl.ca /staticfiles/PublicWebsite/Home/ResearchPublications/BackgroundPapers/PDF/2009-20-e.pdf on August 10, 2021.

Carney, L. D. (Producer), Atlas, J. (Director, cowriter), & Morris, M. W. (Cowriter). (2019). *Pushout: The criminalization of Black girls in schools* [Motion picture]. Los Angeles, CA: Women in the Room Productions.

Centers for Disease Control and Prevention. (2016). Sexual identity, sex of sexual contacts, and health-related behaviors among students in grades 9–12—United States and selected sites, 2015. *Morbidity and Mortality Weekly Report, 65*(9). Accessed at www.cdc.gov/mmwr/volumes/65/ss /pdfs/ss6509.pdf on April 1, 2021.

Centers for Disease Control and Prevention. (2021, April 19). *Health equity considerations and racial and ethnic minority groups.* Accessed at www.cdc.gov/coronavirus/2019-ncov/community/health-equity/race-ethnicity.html on June 15, 2021.

Centre for Justice & Reconciliation. (n.d.). *What is restorative justice?* Accessed at http://restorativejustice.org/#sthash.SyhgIgNE.dpbs on April 1, 2021.

Cincinnati Public Schools. (2017, February 27). *Equity and excellence in education.* Accessed at www.cps-k12.org/sites/www.cps-k12.org/files/pdfs/boe-2255-Policy-Equity-and-Excellence-in-Education-5-10-2018.pdf on September 20, 2021.

Cook, C. R., Fiat, A., Larson, M., Daikos, C., Slemrod, T., Holland, E. A., et al. (2018). Positive greetings at the door: Evaluation of a low-cost, high-yield proactive classroom management strategy. *Journal of Positive Behavior Interventions, 20*(3), 149–159.

Delpit, L. (2005). *Other people's children: Cultural conflict in the classroom.* New York: New Press.

Delpit, L. (2012). *"Multiplication is for white people": Raising expectations for other people's children.* New York: New Press.

Department for Education. (2021a). *School teacher workforce.* Accessed at www.ethnicity-facts-figures.service.gov.uk/workforce-and-business/workforce-diversity/school-teacher-workforce/latest on August 13, 2021.

Department for Education. (2021b). *Schools, pupils and their characteristics.* Accessed at https://explore-education-statistics.service.gov.uk/find-statistics/school-pupils-and-their-characteristics on August 13, 2021.

Edward M. Kennedy Institute. (2021). *Shirley Chisholm.* Accessed at www.bringyourownchair.org/about-shirley-chisholm/ on April 28, 2021.

Equity and Excellence Commission. (2013). *For each and every child: A strategy for education equity and excellence.* Accessed at www2.ed.gov/about/bdscomm/list/eec/equity-excellence-commission-report.pdf on April 23, 2021.

Eurich, T. (2018, January 4). *What self-awareness really is (and how to cultivate it).* Accessed at https://hbr.org/2018/01/what-self-awareness-really-is-and-how-to-cultivate-it on April 1, 2021.

Every Student Succeeds Act of 2015, Pub. L. No. 114-95, 20 U.S.C. § 1177 (2015).

Falk, G., Romero, P. D., Carter, J. A., Nicchitta, I. A., & Nyhof, E. C. (2021, June 15). *Unemployment rates during the COVID-19 pandemic.* Accessed at https://fas.org/sgp/crs/misc/R46554.pdf on August 11, 2021.

Fernandez, L. (2016, April 21). *Empathy and social justice: The power of proximity in improvement science* [Blog post]. Accessed at www.carnegiefoundation.org/blog/empathy-and-social-justice-the-power-of-proximity-in-improvement-science/ on April 26, 2021.

GCFGlobal. (n.d.). *What is an echo chamber?* Accessed at https://edu.gcfglobal.org/en/digital-media-literacy/what-is-an-echo-chamber/1 on June 15, 2021.

Gorski, P. C. (1999). *A brief history of multicultural education.* Accessed at www.edchange.org/multicultural/papers/edchange_history.html on August 10, 2021.

Grimm v. Gloucester County School Board, No. 19-1952 4d Cir. (2020). Accessed at www.ca4.uscourts.gov/opinions/191952.P.pdf on August 16, 2021.

Hammond, Z. (2015). *Culturally responsive teaching and the brain: Promoting authentic engagement and rigor among culturally and linguistically diverse students.* Thousand Oaks, CA: Corwin Press.

Heifetz, R., Grashow, A., & Linsky, M. (2009). *The practice of adaptive leadership: Tools and tactics for changing your organization and the world.* Boston: Harvard Business Press.

Heifetz, R., & Laurie, D. L. (1997). The work of leadership. *Harvard Business Review, 75*(1), 124–134.

Hinde, E. R. (2004). *School culture and change: An examination of the effects of school culture on the process of change.* Accessed at www.researchgate.net/publication/251297989_School_Culture _and_Change_An_Examination_of_the_Effects_of_School_Culture_on_the_Process_of_Change on April 1, 2021.

Hinkson, L. (2015). *Racial issues in urban schools* [Video file]. Accessed at www.youtube.com /watch?v=DNs3HDMp9hA on August 10, 2021.

International Institute for Restorative Practices. (n.d.). *Defining restorative.* Accessed at www.iirp .edu/defining-restorative/5-2-circles on April 29, 2021.

Jefferson, T. (1784). *Notes on the state of Virginia.* Accessed at https://search.lib.virginia.edu/sources /uva_library/items/u1768743 on April 23, 2021.

Jefferson, T. (1814). *Letter from Thomas Jefferson to Peter Carr (September 7, 1814).* Accessed at https://encyclopediavirginia.org/entries/letter-from-thomas-jefferson-to-peter-carr-september -7-1814/ on October 20, 2020.

Kendi, I. X. (2019). *How to be an antiracist.* New York: One World.

Kirwan Institute for the Study of Race and Ethnicity. (2012, May 29). *Understanding implicit bias.* Accessed at https://kirwaninstitute.osu.edu/article/understanding-implicit-bias on April 28, 2021.

Kohli, R., Pizarro, M., & Nevárez, A. (2017). The "new racism" of K–12 schools: Centering critical research on racism. *Review of Research in Education, 41*(1), 182–202.

Ladson-Billings, G. (1995). Toward a theory of culturally relevant pedagogy. *American Educational Research Journal, 32*(3), 465–491.

Ladson-Billings, G. (2009). *The dreamkeepers: Successful teachers of African American children* (2nd ed.). San Francisco: Jossey-Bass.

Ladson-Billings, G. (2021). I'm here for the hard re-set: Post pandemic pedagogy to preserve our culture. *Equity and Excellence in Education, 54*(1). Accessed at www.tandfonline.com/doi/full/10.1 080/10665684.2020.1863883 on August 11, 2021.

Learning for Justice. (2017). *Responding to hate and bias at school: A guide for administrators, counselors, and teachers.* Accessed at www.learningforjustice.org/magazine/publications/responding -to-hate-and-bias-at-school on June 3, 2021.

Learning for Justice. (2018). *How to be an ally.* Accessed at www.learningforjustice.org/magazine /spring-2018/how-to-be-an-ally on July 8, 2021.

Lewis, C. M., DuBow, W. M., & McMullen, K. (2019). Leading conversations about microaggressions, bias, and other difficult topics. *SIGCSE*, 805–806.

Lindsey, D. B., Lindsey, R. B., & Martinez, R. S. (2006). *Culturally proficient coaching: Supporting educators to create equitable schools.* Thousand Oaks, CA: Corwin Press.

Lorde, A. (1997). *The collected poems of Audre Lorde.* New York: Norton.

Love, B. L. (2019). *We want to do more than survive: Abolitionist teaching and the pursuit of educational freedom*. Boston: Beacon Press.

Mapp, K., & Bergman, E. (2019). *Dual capacity-building framework for family-school partnerships (version 2)*. Accessed at www.dualcapacity.org on July 9, 2021.

Mascareñaz, L. (2017, September 8). *Beyond family engagement: Toward the "open system"* [Blog post]. Accessed at https://apluscolorado.org/blog/moving-beyond-family-engagement-toward-open-system on April 1, 2021.

Mascareñaz, L. (2018, November 16). *Teachers! Repeat after me: I will not have my students make "Indian" feathers/clothes. I will not culturally appropriate an entire people for "cute" activities. I will tell my students the truth about this country's relationship with Indigenous people*. Accessed at https://twitter.com/laurynmaria/status/1063526836708216835 on July 9, 2021.

McArdle, N., & Acevedo-Garcia, D. (2017, April). *Consequences of segregation for children's opportunity and wellbeing*. Paper presented at A Shared Future: Fostering Communities of Inclusion in an Era of Inequality, a national symposium hosted by the Harvard Joint Center for Housing Studies, Cambridge, MA.

McVee, M. B., Dunsmore, K., & Gavelek, J. R. (2005). Schema theory revisited. *Review of Educational Research, 75*(4), 531–566.

Motamedi, J. G., & Stevens, D. (2018). *Human resources practices for recruiting, selecting, and retaining teachers of color*. Accessed at https://ies.ed.gov/ncee/edlabs/regions/northwest/pdf/human-resources-practices.pdf on April 1, 2021.

Move to End Violence. (2016, September 7). *Ally or co-conspirator?: What it means to act #InSolidarity* [Blog post]. Accessed at https://movetoendviolence.org/blog/ally-co-conspirator-means-act-insolidarity on April 1, 2021.

National Assessment of Educational Progress (n.d.). *Achievement gaps*. Accessed at https://nces.ed.gov/nationsreportcard/studies/gaps/ on August 13, 2021.

National Association for Multicultural Education. (n.d.). *What is equity?* Accessed at www.nameorg.org/learn/what_is_equity.php on April 1, 2021.

National Center for Education Statistics. (2021, May). *English language learners in public schools*. Accessed at https://nces.ed.gov/programs/coe/indicator_cgf.asp on June 15, 2021.

National Equity Project. (n.d.). *National Equity Project definition of educational equity*. Accessed at www.nationalequityproject.org/education-equity-definition on April 23, 2021.

Ndaruhutse, S., Jones, C., & Riggall, A. (2019). *Why systems thinking is important for the education sector* [Report]. Accessed at https://files.eric.ed.gov/fulltext/ED603263.pdf on August 10, 2021.

North, A. (2020, June 3). *What it means to be anti-racist*. Accessed at www.vox.com/2020/6/3/21278245/antiracist-racism-race-books-resources-antiracism on April 23, 2021.

Noy, D. (2008). Power mapping: Enhancing sociological knowledge by developing generalizable analytical public tools. *The American Sociologist, 39*(1), 3–18. Accessed at www.jstor.org/stable/41217764 on August 4, 2021.

Oluo, I. (2019). *So you want to talk about race*. New York: Seal Press.

Oregon Department of Education. (2020, October 15). *Black Lives Matter resolution*. Accessed at www.oregon.gov/ode/students-and-family/equity/SchoolSafety/Documents/Black%20Lives%20Matter%20Resolution%20October%2015.pdf on September 20, 2021.

Orfield, G., & Eaton, S. E. (1997). *Dismantling desegregation: The quiet reversal of Brown v. Board of Education*. New York: The New Press.

Orfield, G., & Frankenberg, E. (2014). *Brown at 60: Great progress, a long retreat and an uncertain future*. Accessed at https://civilrightsproject.ucla.edu/research/k-12-education/integration-and -diversity/brown-at-60-great-progress-a-long-retreat-and-an-uncertain-future on April 1, 2021.

Organisation for Economic Co-operation and Development. (2012). *Equity and quality in education: Supporting disadvantaged students and schools*. Paris: OECD Publishing. Accessed at www.oecd.org/education/school/50293148.pdf on June 7, 2021.

Peters, M. A. (2015). Why is my curriculum white? *Educational Philosophy and History, 47*(7), 641–646.

Piaget, J., & Inhelder, B. (1969). *The psychology of the child* (2nd ed., H. Weaver, Trans.). New York: Basic Books.

Race Forward: The Center for Racial Justice Innovation. (2006, April 13). *Historical timeline of public education in the U. S.* Accessed at www.raceforward.org/research/reports/historical-timeline -public-education-us on April 1, 2021.

Riddle, T., & Sinclair, S. (2019). Racial disparities in school-based disciplinary actions are associated with county-level rates of racial bias. *Proceedings of the National Academy of Sciences of the United States of America, 116*(17), 8255–8260.

Roy, A. (2020, April 3). *The pandemic is a portal*. Accessed at www.ft.com/content/10d8f5e8-74eb -11ea-95fe-fcd274e920ca on April 23, 2021.

Ryan, J., Pollock, K., & Antonelli, F. (2007). *Teacher and administrator diversity in Canada: Leaky pipelines, bottlenecks and glass ceilings*. Paper presented at the Annual Conference of the Society for the Study of Education, Saskatoon, Saskatchewan, Canada. Accessed at http://home.oise. utoronto.ca/~jryan/pub_files/Art.April09.numbers.pdf on August 13, 2021.

Schott Foundation for Public Education. (2009). *Lost opportunity: A 50 state report on the opportunity to learn in America*. Accessed at http://schottfoundation.org/sites/default/files/resources/50_state _report_national_summary_0.pdf on April 1, 2021.

Scialabba, N. (2019). *How bias impacts our children in education*. Accessed at www.americanbar.org /groups/litigation/committees/childrens-rights/articles/2017/fall2017-how-implicit-bias-impacts -our-children-in-education/ on August 10, 2021.

Seneca. (1920). *Ad lucilium epistulae morales* (R. M. Gummere, Trans.). London: Heinemann.

Senge, P. M., & Sterman, J. D. (1992). Systems thinking and organizational learning: Acting locally and thinking globally in the organization of the future. *European Journal of Operational Research, 59*(1), 137–150.

Sharma, A., Joyner, A. M., & Osment, A. (2014). Adverse impact of racial isolation on student performance: A study in North Carolina. *Education Policy Analysis Archives, 22*(14). Accessed at https://epaa.asu.edu/ojs/article/view/1354/1221 on June 15, 2021.

Singleton, G. E. (2015). *Courageous conversations about race: A field guide for achieving equity in schools* (2nd ed.). Thousand Oaks, CA: Corwin Press.

Stone, N. (2017). *Dear Martin*. New York: Crown.

Thomas, A. (2017). *The hate u give*. New York: Balzer + Bray.

Torres, K., & Massey, D. S. (2012). Fitting in: Segregation, social class, and the experiences of black students at selective colleges and universities. *Race and social problems*, *4*(3–4), 171–192.

Tran, K. (2016, May 2). *5 simple questions that'll help you avoid unintentional cultural appropriation.* Accessed at https://everydayfeminism.com/2016/05/avoid-cultural-appropriation/ on April 29, 2021.

U.S. Department of Education. (2016, July). *The state of racial diversity in the educator workforce.* Accessed at www2.ed.gov/rschstat/eval/highered/racial-diversity/state-racial-diversity-workforce.pdf on April 1, 2021.

U.S. Department of Education. (2019, February). *Status and trends in the education of racial and ethnic groups 2018* (NCES 2019-038). Accessed at https://nces.ed.gov/pubs2019/2019038.pdf on April 1, 2021.

Winfrey, O. (n.d.). *The powerful lesson Maya Angelou taught Oprah.* Accessed at www.oprah.com /oprahs-lifeclass/the-powerful-lesson-maya-angelou-taught-oprah-video on April 29, 2021.

World Bank. (2021, June 8). *The global economy: On track for strong but uneven growth as COVID-19 still weighs.* Accessed at www.worldbank.org/en/news/feature/2021/06/08/the-global-economy-on -track-for-strong-but-uneven-growth-as-covid-19-still-weighs on August 11, 2021.

INDEX

Beyond Conversations About Race
Washington Collado, Sharroky Hollie, Rosa Isiah,
Yvette Jackson, Anthony Muhammad, Douglas Reeves,
and Kenneth C. Williams
Written by a collective of brilliant authors, this essential work
provokes respectful dialogue about race that catalyzes school-
changing action. The book masterfully weaves together an array
of scenarios, discussions, and challenging topics to help prepare
all of us to do better in our schools and communities.
BKG035

Finding Your Blind Spots
Hedreich Nichols
Author Hedreich Nichols infuses this book with a direct yet
conversational style to help you identify biases that adversely
affect your practice and learn how to move beyond those biases
to ensure a more equitable, inclusive campus culture.
BKG022

Dismantling a Broken System
Zachary Wright
Become a hyperlocal activist for change and help ensure
a bright future for every student. Written for educators at
all levels, this resource dives into the American education
system, exposing the history of discrimination and offering
strategies for establishing financially and academically
equitable learning environments.
BKG015

Supporting Underserved Students
Sharroky Hollie and Daniel Russell, Jr.
Discover a clear two-step roadmap for aligning PBIS with
culturally and linguistically responsive teaching. First, you'll
dive deep into *why* there is an urgent need for this alignment
and then learn *how* to move forward to better serve all
learners, especially those from historically underserved
populations.
BKG010

Solution Tree | Press

a division of
Solution Tree

Visit SolutionTree.com or call 800.733.6786 to order.